Michael Barry

VICTORIAN DUBLIN REVEALED
The Remarkable Legacy of Nineteenth-Century Dublin

Andalus Press

Published with support from

and Iarnród Éireann

Published by Andalus Press
7 Frankfort Avenue, Rathgar, Dublin 6
Ireland
www.andalus.ie
info@andalus.ie

By the same author:
Across Deep Waters, Bridges of Ireland
Restoring a Victorian House
Through the Cities, the Revolution in Light Rail
Homage to al-Andalus, the Rise and Fall of Islamic Spain
Tales of the Permanent Way, Stories from the Heart of Ireland's Railways

Jacket: cover photographs, Michael Barry
Back flap: author photograph, Veronica Barry
Endpapers: Panorama of Dublin, *Illustrated London News*, 1846

Jacket design by Anú Design
Book design by Michael Barry

Printed by Printer Trento S.r.l. Italy

ISBN 978-0-9560383-2-6

Contents

Acknowledgements & Illustrations   5

Preface   7

Chapter 1   The Age of Victoria   9

Chapter 2   The Beckoning Suburbs   49

Chapter 3   Mind and Soul   81

Chapter 4   The Wheels of Industry   117

Chapter 5   The Well-Connected City   159

Bibliography   189

Index   190

For Veronica Barry

Acknowledgements

I was privileged to be allowed to see and photograph the hidden parts of Victorian Dublin. This experience proved to me that, in essence, people are very kind. I am grateful to the following people who gave me invaluable assistance in the course of preparing this book:

Tom Coffey and David Brennan of the Dublin City Business Association gave me enthusiastic support. Thanks are also due to: Barry Kenny and Richard Fearon, Iarnród Éireann; John Tierney, Dublin City Manager; Michael Smith, Institute of Advanced Studies; Dave McLynn, Bus Éireann; Ciara Quinn, CIÉ; Siobhán Fitzpatrick, RIA; Olivia Waters and Paul Ferguson, TCD; Mary McGovern and Emma Wilde, Ulster Bank; Damian Ryan, Doheny & Nesbitts; Marcus Houlihan, The Long Hall; Eric Lavelle, Ger Goodwin and Ned Fleming of Dublin City Council; Angela O'Connell, Dublin City Library; Sammie Appleyard, AIB; Simon Fullam, Caroline Douglas and Finbar O'Brian, NIB; Breda Melvin, O'Brien Institute, Marino; Derek Lambe, Department of Foreign Affairs; Aoife McBride, National Museum; Nigel Monaghan, Natural History Museum; Louise Morgan, National Gallery; Róisín Iremonger, Gaiety Theatre; Denis McCarthy of the OPW, Dublin Castle; Greg Harkin of All Hallows; Michael Corcoran of the National Transport Museum; Eibhlin Roche, Archivist, Diageo; Gemma Nolan and Harriet Wheelock of the Royal College of Physicians of Ireland.

I am grateful to the Defence Forces for allowing me access to the Dublin army barracks; in particular thanks are due to Captain Pat O'Connor and Commandant John O'Loughlin, Lieutenant David O'Brien (Cathal Brugha Barracks) and, Commandant Barry Carey and Lieutenant Vincent McGrath (McKee Barracks).

Gerry Nyhan of the Alliance Française showed me the hidden splendours of the former Kildare Street Club. Rebecca Hayes showed me the remarkable architecture of the Freemasons' Hall in Molesworth Street. Niall Dardis and Breda Daly of Dublin Port, were helpful and Charlie McCarthy kindly arranged for a voyage by launch to Victorian parts of the port for me and my daughter Olivia. Thanks to my friend Dermot O'Doherty who accompanied me on several expeditions around Victorian Dublin. We enjoyed being shown around Dublin Zoo by the Director, Leo Oosterweghel. Dermot, along with Michael Forde, Frank Twoomey, Tony McGettigan and Phillip Pearson formed a 'Council of State' which gave valuable advice at key junctures of this project. Paddy Sammon kindly reviewed my work and contributed enormously. Daltún Ó Ceallaigh, as usual, steadfastly supported my quest for perfect grammar, but all errors are mine.

Finally, I am indebted to my wife Veronica. She provided me with continuous support and guided me throughout. She possesses the Victorian attributes of industry, diligence and belief in progress with the more modern virtue of being able to sparkle with improving ideas.

Illustrations

The map of Dublin on page 10 is courtesy of the Map Library, Trinity College Library, University of Dublin.

All photographs in this book are by Michael Barry. His photographs of the National Library, National Gallery, National Museum and Natural History Museum are courtesy of these insitutions and copyright is vested with these. The other photographs in this book are copyright of Michael Barry.

Dublin's Giraldas

Seville has its Giralda, the soaring minaret of a former mosque from the time of al-Andalus. In Victorian Dublin, towers were very popular, albeit not of the same historical significance. Below, (clockwise from top left) is a small selection: St. Anne's, St. Ita's Portrane, McGeough Home, Farmleigh, Masonic Girls' School and Rathmines Town Hall.

Preface

It is a curious fact that many people do not realise the full extent and significance of Victorian times. This is, perhaps, because it is all around us. For those of us in Dublin, we engage with it daily and as a result much of the Victorian city has merged into the background of everyday life. Many (lucky) people live in a Victorian house, residing in those nineteenth-century suburbs that form a red-brick necklace around the central city. Numerous people work in an office, bank or other location that was built in Victorian times. All use the infrastructure of the Victorian era, such as water supply, drainage, bridges and the railways. Electricity and the telephone were introduced towards the end of Victoria's reign. The chances are that you worship in a Victorian church, given that so many of these were constructed during the surge in nineteenth-century church building. Those 63 years of Victoria's reign spanned the peak of the industrial revolution. The pattern of life changed enormously. For Dublin, those were the formative years in which were created the foundations of the modern city.

It was only when I began work on this book that I began to fully comprehend the remarkable extent of the Victoriana that we still have in Dublin. There are probably more remains of that era in Dublin than in most comparable cities. I hope that readers will agree when they see, described in this book, the wealth of buildings from that time still in place. Dublin boasts not just a vast array of nineteenth-century houses and fine buildings and churches but also the more functional elements, such as railway stations, bridges and reservoirs. We are privileged to inherit this intriguing and unique legacy.

The Victorian era in Dublin has not been accorded its due attention. It has been overshadowed by the understandable attention paid to the Georgian city. As it happens, Dublin Victorian architecture retained a fundamental classical style during the initial years and there is a unity and a continuity between the Georgian and early Victorian areas of the city. With both Georgian and Victorian architecture, there was, in certain circles, the feeling that this was not part of Ireland's heritage. In Frank McDonald's book, *The Destruction of Dublin,* he relates how a cabinet minister in 1957 said, concerning the demolition of two Georgian houses, 'I was glad to see them go. They stood for everything I hate.' Thankfully, attitudes have changed since those times. Victorian Dublin is fully part of the mosaic that makes up Irish heritage and is worthy of attention in its own right. It too needs to be appreciated, with tours of important buildings and areas, and to share in conservation measures, including financial support into the future. I hope that this book will contribute somewhat towards redressing the balance through setting out the extensive legacy of this time.

The term 'Victorian' is useful to define a period when significant change occurred in Ireland and particularly in Dublin. Victoria enjoyed a long reign, so a lot happened. There was discernible change in architectural styles over that period and a move away from the classical styles of the early nineteenth century. This book is not set strictly in the period of Victoria's reign from 1837 to 1901. There is a small overlap into the periods before and after, as trends in history and architecture do not begin or end in such a rigid manner.

The nineteenth century was a time of major change for Ireland's capital. At the beginning of that century, following the Act of Union, it endured the shock of losing its parliament and status. Despite the danger of it becoming a mere provincial city, Dublin avoided this and maintained a sense of being something more. The city, for various reasons, did not grow very much as an industrial centre. Consequently, it developed at a snail's pace in comparison to the Birminghams and the Belfasts of that time. In terms of size, it slipped from being the second city of the Empire into a mere tenth place by the century's end. However, it became the country's administrative, financial, commercial and cultural centre. Furthermore, it became the main transport hub of Ireland, adorned with five railway termini and excellent railway connections to the rest of the country. The steamship brought the benefits of easy connections across the Irish Sea. However, it also brought competition to local industry, arising from the now easy access for British manufactured goods.

Dublin developed differently, in comparison to other nineteenth-century cities. It was at the centre of the peculiar mix of politics and religion that prevailed in Ireland at that time. Post-Emancipation Catholicism, along with nationalism, was on the rise. The dominant Protestant ascendancy and middle class were on the back foot as they began to experience a gradual waning of their power and influence. In tandem with this, the middle class began to flee to the new suburbs, against the background of a declining central city. This peculiar combination of religion, class and nationalism had an influence on aspects of Dublin's geography and environment such as the development of the suburbs and the rapid building of assertive churches.

Victorian Dublin was generally a comfortable place for the middle class, ensconced in its expanding suburbs. Life in a place like Rathmines, assuming one had the necessary income, was not much different from that of a comparable middle-class suburb in London, albeit with rawer sectarian tensions seething below the surface. The attitudes and mores were similar. Victorians entertained a spirit of hope and progress. New inventions were continually rolled out. Consumer goods, the fruits of the large factories of northern England, were readily available in the shops and in the 'Monster Stores' of Grafton Street and surrounds.

However, life was different for the poor. Whether in the congested old districts of the Liberties, or in the newly-tenemented parts of the old Georgian north city, conditions were appalling with squalor and disease prevalent. It would be only later in the nineteenth century that practical initiatives, such as a potable water supply, drainage and housing for the working class, were introduced.

The Victorian city embodied a curious mixture of decline, comfort and squalor. Uniquely in the nineteenth century, Dublin was at the intersection of two worlds: the one of its hinterland – colonial Ireland, poor and predominantly Catholic; the other – one of the important administrative and commercial cities of the United Kingdom. The Dublin middle class aspired to the values of Victorian Britain and engaged enthusiastically with its empire as soldiers and civil servants. This is illustrated poignantly in places such as St. Patrick's Cathedral, full of monuments to young Irishmen who joined the British forces and fought and died in the wars of imperial conquest.

Intrigued by this piquant story of Victorian Dublin and the promise of its visible heritage, I set off on my exploration of the city during the 1980s. Roaming far and wide, I took photographs as I went and delved into its history. Diverted by other matters (not least a book on restoring a Victorian house) this work was set aside for two decades. I restarted my efforts to capture nineteenth-century Dublin a few years ago, now armed with a digital camera. These efforts are displayed in this book: photographs of the old city as it exists in the twenty-first century, but also some from over 30 years ago. Many of the older photographs show buildings that have been demolished or, like the Point Depot, radically changed.

This book is not intended as a formal tome on Victorian architecture in Dublin. Rather, it is a personal, perhaps idiosyncratic, evocation of the spirit of Victorian Dublin portrayed through photographs of what remains. Woven into all of this is the story of the city during that fascinating era, a time of great societal change. Above all, this book is meant to reveal the remarkable legacy of Victorian Dublin in an entertaining manner so, dear reader, please enjoy it.

Chapter 1
The Age of Victoria

The Victorian Age in Dublin was a whirlwind of competing forces in politics, class and religion. These were in play against the background of the advancing Industrial Revolution and radical change in Ireland and the outside world. Once the second city of the Empire, Dublin experienced mixed fortunes during Victoria's reign. However, it was the buildings and institutions developed during that time, no less than those during the Georgian era, which were to give the city the critical mass to be a true European capital upon gaining independence in 1922.

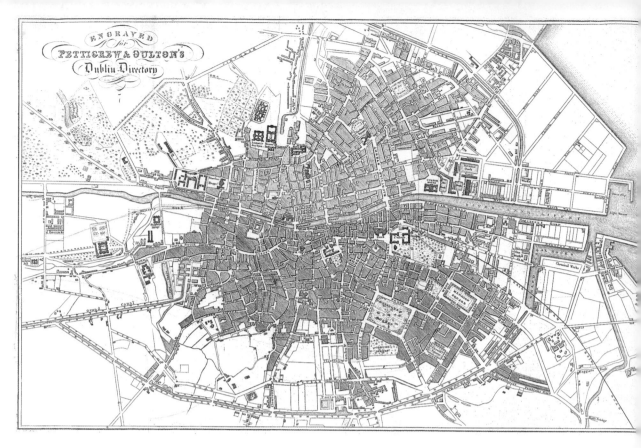

Engraved for PETTIGREW & OULTON'S Dublin Directory

Above. Dublin in 1834.

In the opening decades of the nineteenth century, Europe was at the heart of the developed world. When the Napoleonic Wars ended, the way was clear for a surge in economic development and modernisation, energised by the industrial revolution. This was manifest at the Congress of Vienna (1814-15) where post-war Europe was reorganised. (Incidentally the United Kingdom was represented there by two Dublin-born worthies: Viscount Castlereagh and the first Duke of Wellington, who replaced him.) The victorious United Kingdom of Great Britain and Ireland emerged as the pre-eminent power in Europe. The Napoleonic Wars had devastated much of the continent, while Great Britain had avoided warfare on its territory. The industrial revolution was underway, with machinery replacing many processes done by hand. In turn, water power was being replaced by the steam engine. Britain had a fortuitous abundance of the essentials of the Industrial Revolution, coal and iron ore. The colonies in the West Indies, India and elsewhere provided raw materials and markets. Over the years British society and civil structures had developed into a more sophisticated form, better able to support rapid economic development. When the young Victoria ascended the throne in 1837, the railway age had begun. Up to then, transport had been either by horsepower or by canal. As the railway network spread, transport became accessible, quick and reliable. Factory owners could easily ship their goods all over the country and abroad. Britain became the 'workshop of the world'. As industrial production rose, the population grew rapidly. It was a period of immense social transformation. In addition to the new urban working classes staffing the factories, there was the rise of the middle class, which began to play an increasingly prominent part in society. The Victo-

Right. The Wellington Testimonial Monument, in the Phoenix Park, originally begun in 1817, was completed in 1861. Reputed to be the highest obelisk in Europe, it is a potent reminder of the prominent part Irishmen played in Britain's imperial adventure. It commemorates Arthur Wellesley, first Duke of Wellington. Bronze melted from cannons captured at Waterloo was used for some of the decoration. Plaques depict the Duke's victory at Waterloo and, right, scenes from the Siege of Seringapatam in India, in which he fought.

Left. Pediment on the former Provincial Bank (now the Westin Hotel) on College Street. Commercial activity surrounds the seated maiden. To the left is foreign trade, including an anchor and an African. To the right, agriculture is represented by a beehive, a lamb and wheat.

Middle and below left. Irish Victorian life as depicted in statuary. Details from the O'Connell Monument in what is now the eponymous street. Executed by the leading sculptor, John Henry Foley, and completed in 1883, after Foley's death. The display includes, in the centre, the figure of Erin trampling on her chains, a bishop counselling a youth, a lawyer, artisans and what looks like a royal personage consulting with a statesman.

Right. Arguably the finest statue in Dublin. Prince Albert, by John Henry Foley (1871), at the south end of Leinster Lawn. Tucked away discreetly in hedging, this statue of Victoria's consort has survived the perilous outcomes which affected royal statuary in Dublin. Albert, who died in 1861, was a believer in the Victorian virtues of improvement and progress. This is reflected by the earnest young figures that surround the statue. They represent Art, Manufacturing and Science.

13

In Victorian Dublin, the authorities were watchful for the threat of disorder. The maintenance of law and order was a high priority.

Right. Mountjoy Gaol was designed by Joshua Jebb (knighted in 1859) and dates from 1847-50. It is similar to the radiating layout of the prison in Pentonville, London (also designed by Jebb), then regarded as a pioneering model for prisons.

Left. The striking ironwork of the east wing of Kilmainham Gaol which was extended in 1861 to a design by John McCurdy. The high and spacious galleries are in marked contrast to the cramped spaces of the earlier part of the prison.

Near left. The central police training depot of 1842, at the Phoenix Park, which is now Garda Headquarters.

Far left. The Officers' Mess, designed in a Lombardic style by E. Trevor Owen, which dates from 1863.

Right. Prison at Arbour Hill, originally built as a military prison in 1845-48. Again, Joshua Jebb, the leading expert in prisons, was involved in its design.

Fear of sedition in Ireland resulted in a massive military presence in Dublin. There were many barracks in the city and red coats dotted the streets of the nineteenth-century city.

Above and left. Marlborough (now McKee) Barracks is a delightful late-Victorian confection, still in use as a barracks. The red-brick design with turrets and copper cupolas gives echoes of imperial adventure.

Right. More Victorian red brick (1889), at Islandbridge (Clancy) Barracks, now redeveloped as an apartment complex.

Above. Portobello (now Cathal Brugha) Barracks, of 1815, has many Victorian additions.

Right. Royal (Collins) Barracks dates from 1706. The red brick is ninteenth-century.

rians lived through a period that has been called the most radical transformation ever seen in the world.

The world had become a smaller place, thanks to the railway and the steamship. The unmapped parts of the globe, notably large tracts of Africa, became the subject of an undignified scramble for territory by the European powers later in the nineteenth century. Britain led the way in creating a vast empire, marked notably when Victoria took the title of 'Empress of India' in 1876. However, while Victoria's kingdom was at the dynamic heart of the developed nineteenth-century world, the second element of the kingdom, Ireland, formed an asymmetric part. It was agricultural, poorer, disaffected, and its population predominantly adhered to a religion different from that bedrock of the kingdom, the Established Church.

Ireland, radically dissimilar to the powerful, industrialising island of Britain, in turn had a capital that was different from the rest of the country. Following its foundation as a Viking town, Dublin developed into the centre for control by the neighbouring island over the following centuries. The eighteenth century had been good for the city. With its own parliament and the presence of the landed aristocracy, Dublin experienced unprecedented growth during the second half of that century. The rise in agricultural prices allowed the ascendancy to build the great squares and townhouses of the Georgian city. Dublin by 1800 was the second city of the British Empire and a great city in world terms. It was not as grand as London, Vienna or the other imperial capitals, but was in the front rank of the second cities of Europe. With the passing of the Act of Union in 1800, this all changed. The bubble of the bright, fashionable and wealthy city burst. As the parliamentarians and their entourage packed their bags and left for London, Dublin lost some of the soul and confidence of a capital with its own parliament. At the start of the Victorian age, Dublin was in danger of becoming a provincial city of the United Kingdom. As it turned out, it did grow, but only

In the Victorian era, learned men and women sought to advance the boundaries of science. Above. Dunsink Observatory is the oldest scientific institution in Ireland. This observatory building houses the South twelve-inch telescope of 1868.

Right. The Houghton House of 1898 (now reconstructed) at Dublin Zoo and, below right, the entrance lodge, dating from 1833.
Below. Capital in the Roberts House (1902).

18

Above. The Curvilinear Range building at Glasnevin, mainly constructed by the great Dublin ironmaster, Richard Turner, in the period 1845 to 1869.

Left. Cast iron and glass. Details from Turner's Curvilinear Range building. Turner combined the materials of the Industrial Revolution, now readily available, to form the sublime beauty of this building

Right. The Palm House at Glasnevin, which dates from 1884, was made by Boyd of Glasgow.

to a modest extent and only half-heartedly attended, as we will see later, at the altar of the industrial revolution. This near stasis was thrown into sharp and embarrassing contrast by the extraordinary progress in Britain and in Ulster. Dublin fell from its position as second city of the Empire in 1800 to the tenth rank by the end of the Victorian age in 1901. It did not achieve the stellar growth of such cities as Manchester, Liverpool and Birmingham, which rapidly overtook it in population, industry and wealth. Indignity of indignities, it was even overtaken by Belfast. A modest town at the beginning of the Victorian age, Belfast rode the crest of the Victorian wave, led by the adroit development of its linen and shipbuilding industries.

After the Act of Union, there was a political vacuum in Ireland. The focus of power was London where the 100 new Irish members of parliament now attended. By the 1820s, the demand for Catholic Emancipation, led by Daniel O'Connell, had become a true mass movement. O'Connell successfully harnessed the pent-up frustration of Catholics against discriminatory laws. There

Left. Signs of the Zodiac in the mosaic floor in the entrance hall of the National Museum.

Below. Decorative cast iron in the National Museum.

Left. It is worth lifting one's gaze from the exhibits to observe the glorious cast-iron roof of the National Museum, Kildare Street. Completed in 1890, the National Museum (like the nearby National Library) was designed by the Deanes, père et fils, Thomas Newenham and Thomas Manly Deane.

Right. In the National Museum, the decoration of the exquisite ceramic door-surrounds in gold, blue and white was executed by Burmantofts of Leeds. The wooden carved doors are by Carlo Cambi of Siena. Cambi's carvings adorn a wide range of Dublin buildings including the National Library, the Milltown Wing of the National Gallery and Rathmines Town Hall.

were great demonstrations all across the country. In 1829 the Government capitulated and a Catholic Relief Act became law. O'Connell next campaigned for repeal of the Act of Union. However, O'Connell suffered a setback when he yielded to a Government ban and cancelled a planned 'monster meeting' in Clontarf in 1843. The campaign petered out thereafter. He died in Genoa in 1847. The more militant movement, Young Ireland, took up the mantle of Irish nationalism. Many were middle-class and it included both Catholics and Protestants. Inspired by the 1848 Paris revolution, they attempted an insurrection. Forewarned, the Government flooded Dublin with troops. There were some skirmishes in the countryside and the rising collapsed.

Nationalism, resilient, continued in 1858 with the formation of the Fenian movement. The founders included veterans of the 1848 uprising. The essence of

Above. Restrained in its external style, the Natural History Museum, of 1857, has a rich Victorian interior. It contains an exhilarating confection of stuffed animals, trays of preserved specimens (including a collection of insects by Darwin) and mahogany cabinets. David Livingstone gave the inaugural lecture here.

Right. The Natural History Museum, popularly known as the 'Dead Museum'. A statue of Thomas Heazle Parke is located on the front lawn. Parke was an army surgeon who accompanied the explorer H. M. Stanley during the Emin Pasha relief expedition in Africa in 1887-89.

Below. Detail of plaque on T. H. Parke's statue. Stanley (with cap) can be seen to the right. In the centre Parke is sucking the poison from an arrow-wound in the chest of an expedition member. Parke was the first European to see the Ruwenzori or Mountains of the Moon. When he died in 1893, his coffin was drawn from Dublin Docks on a gun-carriage to Broadstone Station and thence to his native Leitrim.

Fenianism was that the British presence should be removed by force. Despite being infiltrated by informers and strong animosity from Archbishop Cullen and the Catholic bishops, they grew into a sizeable organisation with branches not only in Ireland but also in Britain and North America. The Fenians rose in 1867 and were quickly suppressed. Following skirmishes around Dublin, some rebels who had fled to the mountains to the south of the city were eventually captured.

Constitutional nationalism was to continue against a background of agitation over land tenure in the countryside. Isaac Butt led a group of Irish MPs at Westminster to promote the concept of a Dublin parliament dealing with Irish affairs within the Empire. Charles Stewart Parnell became leader of the Irish Parliamentary Party in 1880. The Government reacted to widespread land agitation with the reforming 1881 Land Act. In October 1881, Parnell was incarcerated in Kilmainham Gaol under the Coercion Laws, but was released in May the following year. Parnell's party captured most Irish seats in the general election of 1885. They allied with the Liberals, who defeated the Conservative government in 1886. The Liberal leader William Gladstone, a latter-day convert to the concept, proposed a Home Rule Bill. His party was not convinced, the Bill was defeated and Gladstone resigned. Parnell's fortunes fell when he was named as co-respondent in Mrs O'Shea's divorce case. His party split. He died in 1891, only 45 years old.

In 1882, members of the Invincibles secret society, using surgical knives, assassinated the Chief Secretary Lord Frederick Cavendish and his Under Secretary as they walked in the Phoenix Park. The revolutionary Irish Republican Brotherhood (IRB) had grown as part of the Fenian tradition of the 1850s. The IRB, although overshadowed by the Parnellite movement, persevered and kept

alive the revolutionary nationalist flame, which was to strongly revive at the beginning of the twentieth century.

While much of the political drama took place across the country, Dublin was where many of the main political leaders lived and had their headquarters and factional newspapers. The absence of an Irish parliament led to Dublin Corporation becoming a substitute, to a certain degree, for national politics. Municipal reform in 1840 resulted in Catholic representation which grew rapidly, bringing a nationalist outlook. The Corporation became an arena for national issues. The Protestant middle class was alienated and this encouraged its retreat to the growing suburbs. This concentration on national politics diverted the Corporation from confronting the city's many problems. In retrospect, its achievements were modest – there are few significant municipal buildings from the nineteenth century. Much of the Corporation's legacy of real importance is literally underground: in the form of water and drainage pipes.

During the nineteenth century, the Catholic Church rose and rose, freed from its penal shackles. The number of priests and other religious rapidly increased. In Dublin another caste also grew rapidly: the civil service and administrators. As always, Dublin was at the heart of British power in Ireland and was the centre for the administration of the island. At the top was the Lord Lieutenant. Political control was in the hands of the Chief Secretary, with his headquarters in Dublin Castle. Over the century, government became more

Above. The search for knowledge: the Reading Room of the National Library in all its Victorian splendour. The Library was completed in 1890, to a design by T. N. and T. M. Deane.

Below. Medicine was at an advanced state in nineteenth-century Dublin. Detail from stained glass at the Royal College of Physicians of Ireland (RCPI) at Kildare Street.

interventionist and active. A centralised professional bureaucracy arose to shoulder the burden.

Art, culture and science were served by several imposing buildings and institutions established during the nineteenth century. The establishment of the Botanic Gardens at Glasnevin resulted in the building of sublime glasshouses there and it gained an international reputation for botany. The Zoological Gardens, located in the Phoenix Park, opened in 1831. In true Victorian mode, it combined science and education and also afforded the Dublin populace the opportunity to see exotic creatures from far away. The wealthy contractor William Dargan, known as the 'Father of Irish Railways', organised the Exhibition of Art and Industry on Leinster Lawn in 1853. He was the driving force behind the establishment of the National Gallery, completed in 1864. Later Victorian additions are the National Library and the National Museum, located on either side of Leinster House.

The Great Famine occurred in 1845-49 when blight attacked the potato, staple diet of the rural masses. The government of the richest nation on earth, in thrall to the prevailing ideology of laissez-faire, took only half-hearted relief measures. This resulted in one of the greatest catastrophes of the century. Death by starvation and disease, along with emigration, meant that the population fell by one fifth between 1845 and 1851. Dublin did not suffer directly the misery that was inflicted on rural Ireland. The consequences for the city were more indirect. Refugees from the stricken countryside filled the city's workhouses. Relief

Left. The Royal Victoria Eye and Ear Hospital on Adelaide Road was built from 1901 onwards to a design by Carroll and Batchelor.

Right. Now closed, the Meath Hospital was built from the 1820s onwards. This graceful Victorian cast-iron veranda, one of a series, allowed patients to take the air.

Right. After Catholic Emancipation, Catholic hospitals were established. These facilitated access to the medical profession for the emergent Catholic middle classes. The Mater Hospital on Eccles Street was set up by the Sisters of Mercy. The building was completed in 1861 to a design by John Bourke.

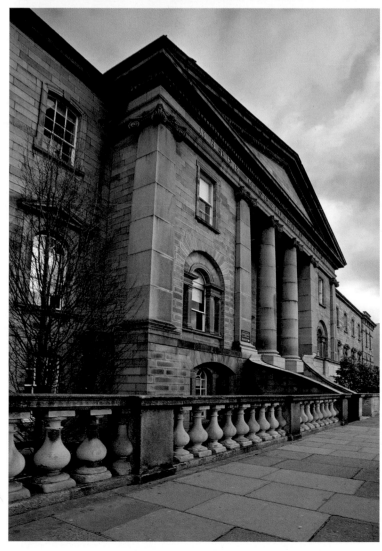

Residences for Nurses, constructed in the ubiquitous red brick:
Far left. A 1980s view of the Nurses' Home of Dr. Steeven's Hospital, now demolished.
Near left. The veranda of the former James Weir Home for Nurses, of 1903, on Cork Street.

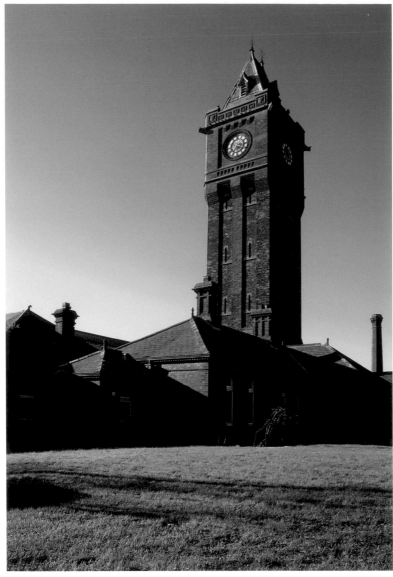

Left. Portrane Asylum (now St. Ita's Hospital) was located on an isolated peninsula, to a design by George Ashlin. Its huge size resulted in a shortage of skilled craftsmen in Dublin during its construction, which commenced in 1896.

Right. The McGeough home for 'elderly ladies of good character' in Cowper Road, Rathmines (1878).

Below left. The former Carmichael School of Medicine, North Brunswick Street. Dating from 1864, the Italian Gothic style included polychrome details around the doors and windows.

Right. Clockwise from near right, late Victorian hospitals: Baggot Street Hospital; Richmond Hospital, with substantial verandas; Dental Hospital at Lincoln Place.

Below. An entrance door of the former Jervis Street hospital. The first blood transfusion in Ireland was carried out there in 1865.

and
soup

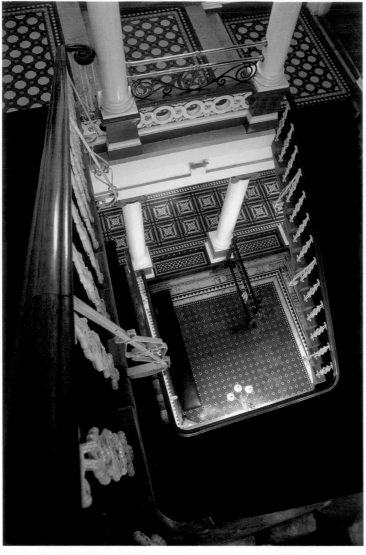

Left. The grand staircase of the Freemasons' Hall, Molesworth Street. The building dates from 1866, designed by Edward Holmes. Within its portals there is an array of exotic rooms, designed around fantastical themes.

Right. The Grand Chapter Room in the Freemasons' Hall. The decoration is in line with the Masonic identification with the priestly rites and rituals of Pharaonic Egypt. The heavy mouldings around the ceiling represent the flora of the Nile.

Below left. Decorative plaque in honour of Queen Victoria, patron of the Order of the Temple.

Below. Gilt decorative detail on column in the Grand Lodge Room.

kitchens were organised across the city. A 'New Model Soup Kitchen' was set up in front of the Royal (now Collins) barracks. A French chef, one Alexis Soyer, devised a special soup potion, made in a huge boiler. The soup was dispensed in bowls to the starving and pauperised, with spoons attached by chain. Despite the calamity affecting the country, the social round continued as before. Plays, concerts and balls amused the gentry. In February 1847, by command of the Lord Lieutenant, the annual Grand Fancy and Full Dress Charity Ball was held in the Rotunda.

While most of the aristocracy had left the city, the social life of Victorian Dublin was continued by the professional and commercial classes. In the season, the Anglo-Irish attended balls and *levées* in Dublin Castle, which included the colourful presence of army officers. Some aspirational Catholics attended these events but sectarian divisions meant that many of the rising Catholic middle class preferred social functions in the Mansion House. The well-to-do could attend horse racing at Punchestown or a military review or polo match in the Phoenix Park. For fresh air they could take the train to the seaside at Blackrock, Kingstown or Bray. They could attend concert performances at the Antient Concert Rooms in Great Brunswick (now Pearse) Street. Theatres included the Royal (burned in 1880) and the Queen's. The Gaiety opened in 1872. Dan Lowry's Music Hall eventually became the Olympia. The Irish literary revival started at the end of the century. Yeats, Synge and Lady Gregory were to the fore and the revival led to the founding of the Abbey Theatre in 1904. There was lively debate in Dublin's newspapers; the city had 24 in 1865. The cause of literacy and knowledge was well served when public libraries were opened in

Above. Mock Gothic abounds in the Prince Masons' Chapter Room.

Right. The Knights Templar Preceptory Room is based on the medieval order of Knights Templars.

Below. Plaques in the Preceptory Room

Left. Memorial plaque in the Freemasons' Hall.

Right. The polychrome red brick of Deane and Woodward's Kildare Street Club (1859-61). The Italianate style is blended with Byzantine. The carved stone detailing is sublime. The building is a suitable red-brick coda to Deane and Woodward's grey limestone masterpiece, the Museum Building just across College Park in Trinity College.

Below right. Monkeys playing billiards – was it a comment by the stone carvers on the rich and leisured denizens of the club?

Below. Meeting Hall of the Royal Irish Academy. The original Georgian house was remodelled and the hall was completed in 1849 to a design by P. C. Hardwick. The cast-iron gallery was supplied by J. & R. Mallet.

1884 in Thomas Street and Capel Street. Lively and literate, Dublin avoided being a mere provincial outlier of Britain. Its piquant social, political and religious mix can be seen as the basis which gave the world the unique viewpoint and literature of such geniuses as James Joyce, Seán O'Casey, Oscar Wilde and George Bernard Shaw, all born in the Victorian city.

The grim conditions of the poor shocked visitors to Dublin. One wrote in 1837 that it was a city of 'lamentable contrasts'. Close to the comfortable homes of the well-to-do were the slums of the poor. Filth, narrow streets and disease proliferated in places such as the Liberties. Beggars abounded. The middle classes fled to the beckoning suburbs, then being developed on the south of the Grand Canal by speculative builders. By the end of the century, and despite the many advances achieved, visitors used to the poverty seen in European cities continued to be shocked by the dirt and decay of Dublin. The poor had moved into many of the grand eighteenth-century townhouses of the gentry, which became slums. Over the nineteenth century, there were frequent outbreaks of cholera and typhoid, which mainly afflicted the poor and occasionally the affluent. The death rate in Dublin was much higher than in comparable British cities. The Victorians believed that noxious odours caused disease. The stench from the Liffey was thought to be a prime cause of a cholera epidemic in 1866. As the century progressed, better understanding of the causes of disease resulted in improvements eventually being made, such as the provision of potable water and effective drainage.

The nineteenth century saw the rise of the professions. Amongst others, to the forefront were the engineers who oversaw the great engineering projects of the time. Many of these remarkable men worked in Dublin. Charles Blacker Vignoles directed the building of the Dublin and Kingstown Railway that opened at the end of 1834. The flat-bottomed rail that he developed is now the standard for railways worldwide. He worked on many foreign projects including

railways in the north of Spain and a chain bridge over the Dnieper in Tsarist Kiev. Perhaps the most exotic of his projects was the proposal for a cast-iron colonnade to be built alongside the Liffey quays to carry trains to connect to the West. Other pioneering engineers of the era included Sir John Macneill (railways), Richard Griffith (Griffith's Valuation and constructing roads in the south-west); Bindon Blood Stoney (docks) and Parke Neville (water and drainage). The nineteenth-century surge in the building of churches and banks gave the architectural profession much employment. This busy workload helped Irish architects gain a reputation among their peers in Britain. These included Sir Thomas Deane and Benjamin Woodward, designers of the splendid Museum Building in Trinity College, as well as the nearby Kildare Street Club. They also designed the Oxford University Museum.

As Dublin grew during the eighteenth century, many hospitals were built. These included Swift's St. Patrick's, Dr. Steevens', Mercer's, the Meath and the Lying-In (later the Rotunda) hospitals. Dublin then had the good fortune of having one of the largest number of hospital beds, per capita, in the United Kingdom. The building of hospitals continued apace during the next century. These included two Catholic teaching hospitals. St. Vincent's was founded in 1834 by the Sisters of Charity. It was located in Georgian buildings on the eastern side of St. Stephen's Green (subsequently vacated by St. Vincent's for the newer pastures of Merrion Road). The Mater Misericordiae Hospital, on Eccles Street, was built for the Sisters of Mercy to a design by John Bourke and opened in 1861. These hospitals were associated with the medical school of the Catholic University and afforded an avenue to a medical career for the rising Catholic middle class. Two other late-Victorian constructions, in vigorous red brick, were the Richmond and Baggot Street hospitals, both now superseded. Despite the prevailing squalor and disease among the city's poor, Dublin, paradoxically, was

Right. Foliage, frozen in time, surrounds an entrance door of the Kildare Street Club. The sublime carving of the white limestone presents a pleasant contrast to the red brick.

Below and right. The floral theme is continued inside the building along the plaster cornices.

Above. The Victorian stained-glass entrance canopy of the Olympia Theatre. The theatre had previously been known as Dan Lowry's.

Left. Plush and richly decorated, the Gaiety Theatre dates from 1871. A spectacle in its own right, it is a delightful example of Victorian theatre, with gilt detail, ornate balconies and groups of colonnaded boxes at either side of the stage.

Lodges were built to accommodate park wardens. Clockwise, from top near right: Gate Lodge at the Blessington Basin in the north inner city; detail from Gate Lodge at Stephen's Green; Lodge in Phoenix Park in rural villa style and with wooden eaves detail; Gate Lodge at Islandbridge Gate, Phoenix Park, part of a series of lodges designed by Decimus Burton in the period 1830-45.

Below. Bandstand in St Stephen's Green erected in 1887 to mark Queen Victoria's Jubilee. It was funded by a subscription by the members of the Dublin Metropolitan Police.

a centre of medical innovation during the nineteenth century. The medical schools of the city established strong reputations (as well as providing a ready market for Dublin's grave-robbers during the first decades of the century). There had been a large number of Irish surgeons in the army and navy during the Napoleonic Wars. These underlying strengths, together with the opportunities arising from the large number of hospitals in the city, resulted in medicine in Victorian Dublin being of a high standard. Sir William Wilde (father of Oscar) was a pioneer in eye surgery. He founded St. Mark's Ophthalmic Hospital in 1844. This, together with the Eye and Ear Infirmary in Molesworth Street, were amalgamated to form the Royal Victoria Eye and Ear Hospital. This splendid structure, on Adelaide Road, was built at the end of the Victorian era. Other Dublin medical pioneers include Francis Rynd who gave the first hypodermic injection in 1844. Robert Adams identified the importance of disorders in cardiac rhythms. The first book on the stethoscope in English was authored by William Stokes who also wrote treatises on cardiac and pulmonary medicine. The surgeon R. McDonnell gave the first blood transfusion in Ireland in 1865 at the Jervis Street Hospital. Sir Dominic Corrigan was a pioneer in heart problems. He advised on medical measures during the Famine and, in 1859, was the first Catholic president of the Royal College of Physicians of Ireland.

The British Government kept Dublin under tight control during the nineteenth century. Order on the streets was maintained by the unarmed Dublin Metropolitan Police, established in 1836. This was backed up by a strong British army presence in Dublin and Ireland in general. In 1826, of the 83 regiments of the line, 23 were garrisoned in Ireland. In the last quarter of the nineteenth century, around 25,000 troops were stationed in the country. There were several reasons for this large presence: a wary precaution against Irish insurrection as

Above. Kingstown was a Victorian seaside resort. During the summer months bands played nearly every evening at this bandstand on the East Pier, at Dún Laoghaire, dating from around 1900.

Left. Classicism in Kingstown, as designed by John Skipton Mulvany. The Royal Irish Yacht Club, in Dún Laoghaire, completed in 1850. The club was founded in 1831 and the first Duke of Wellington was one of the early club members.

Vestiges of Victoria:

Far left. Reproduction cast-iron Victoria Fountain monument in Dún Laoghaire, with the stern-faced monarch's head much in evidence. The original monument was erected to mark the Queen's visit to the then Kingstown in 1900. It replaces the original which was destroyed in 1982.

Near left. Postboxes in cast iron, embellished with the initials of Victoria Regina, were located all over Ireland, visible markers of her imperial rule. Green was the colour of early Victorian postboxes. From the 1870s onwards they were painted red throughout the United Kingdom. In Ireland, once again, the colour is green.

well as an opportunity to recruit in Ireland. The Irish participation in the army was huge: it amounted to around 40% by the time of Victoria's accession. As the Irish population declined as a percentage of that of the United Kingdom, however, the proportion of Irish in the army declined to around 12% by the end of the nineteenth century. Dublin was at the hub of military Ireland, with up to half of the Irish garrison stationed there. Parades, reviews, red coats in the streets, genteel housing for officers in Rathmines, busy brothels – there was a palpable military presence all over the city. The soldiers of Victoria were based in eight barracks dotted around the city. Still in military use are Portobello (now Cathal Brugha) Barracks in Rathmines and Marlborough Barracks (now McKee) on Blackhorse Avenue. The latter is a marvellous example of late-Victorian architecture. An eclectic mix of turrets, great chimney-stacks and a multitude of dormer windows which blend together successfully. Surprisingly, the design of this exhilarating group of buildings emerged from the staid offices of the Royal Engineers' Department in Britain. The overwhelming combination of pinnacled red brick and details like the green copper cupolas gives echoes of imperial adventures and the Raj. The story that the drawings were inadvertently sent to Dublin instead of India is apocryphal.

Queen Victoria's last visit to Dublin in April 1900 was a lenghty one. Long neglect of Ireland meant she had not been to the city for 39 years, but this time she stayed in the Vice-Regal lodge for three weeks. The purpose of her visit was ostensibly to thank the Irish troops who had participated in the South African (Boer) War, as she stated 'to see again the motherland of those brave sons who have recently borne themselves in defence of my Crown and Empire with a cheerful valour.' The nationalists said it was to encourage recruitment to the British Army, still embroiled in the war. During her stay there were the usual dutiful visits to institutions and receptions for local worthies. However, she did travel widely around districts of the city. What changes did she see beyond the welcoming decorations? The signs and bunting spread all over the city were still fulsomely loyal. As the Hanoverian monarch travelled in her coaches along the streets, she would have seen the villas and terraced houses in the affluent south side of the city. She travelled through Drumcondra and would have seen houses built in recent decades for the clerical classes. The carriage would have clattered over the tracks of the extensive Dublin tram network. In the central area around College Green, she could observe a plethora of banks. New churches all over the

Right. Construction of the great harbour at Dunleary commenced in 1817. The town was renamed Kingstown following King George IV's visit in 1821. The East Pier lighthouse was completed in 1842 and the battery completed in 1858. Victoria departed from here in 1900 on the yacht 'Victoria and Albert.' It was her fourth and last visit to Ireland. She died nine months later.

city, mostly Catholic, were there in full prominence. At the end of her stay she travelled on the coastal railway to the royal yacht *Victoria and Albert* moored in Kingstown harbour. It is unlikely that she was overly cognisant of the febrile mix swirling under the surface of the city: Catholicism ascendant versus beleaguered Protestantism; militant nationalism on the rise; uneasy unionists; squalid tenements in the city centre versus leafy middle-class suburbs. Dubliners have an incurable weakness for royalty and the visit was regarded as successful. The aged Queen (she died nine months later) would not have had any premonition of the Dublin rebellion that was to occur against the Empire within 16 years. She departed and the new century rolled on. In retrospect, Dublin, once the second city of the Empire, had experienced mixed fortunes during her reign. However, it was the buildings and institutions developed during that time, no less than those established during the Georgian era, which were to give the city the critical mass to be a true European capital on independence in 1922.

Chapter 2

The Beckoning Suburbs

The suburbs of Dublin emerged during the nineteenth century. As the century progressed the middle classes migrated from the central city to burgeoning townships like Rathmines and Pembroke. Speculative builders constructed suitable residences and, in some instances, controlled the townships. Lower rates added to the contentment of the affluent, living in elegant villas and terraces. As public transport improved, the clerical and lower middle classes began to live in outer areas of the townships. As the townships grew, the central city declined.

The great expansion of Dublin in the second half of the eighteenth century was driven by the aristocracy, then enjoying an unprecedented flow of wealth from their estates. Their power overshadowed that of the commercial and financial strata of society, much more than in comparable European cities. Georgian and aristocratic Dublin had experienced the great residential development of the city to the north of the Liffey, principally in the Gardiner Estate and, later on, in the Fitzwilliam Estate to the south. After the departure of the parliamentarians to London following the Act of Union, the once fashionable houses on the north of the city lost their allure. The streets around Fitzwilliam Square became the new site of fashionable residence for the next decades of the early nineteenth century. Around the middle of that century the decline had taken hold and tenements began to appear on the streets on the north side of the city. The poor moved from such congested and decaying areas as the Liberties and transferred to the formerly grand houses of the gentry.

The middle class was small on the eve of the Victorian age. In the post-Union vacuum, with the decline of the aristocracy, one observer bemoaned (perhaps underestimating a little) in a book *New Picture of Dublin*, dating from 1821, that the gentry of the city amounted to a mere 200 families which included attorneys, physicians and clergymen. The majority of the Dublin middle class at the time were Protestant and the nineteenth century saw a huge increase in the Catholic middle class. The interaction of class, religion and politics was to have a very direct bearing on the development of Dublin over the century, as we shall see. After Catholic Emancipation in 1829 and the legislation in 1840 which allowed a wider franchise, power shifted in Dublin Corporation. By the 1840s Protestant big business members were becoming a minority in the Corporation, which began to take on a liberal as well as a nationalist complexion. The professional and upper classes (predominantly Protestant) became disillusioned with this new trend and the fading charms of the central city. They escaped to the new and growing southern suburbs.

Hitherto the suburbs had been small. Barely more than 30,000 people lived in these areas in 1831 as opposed to over 230,000 people living in the city. At the end of the Victorian era in 1901, the city population had grown to 290,000, while the suburbs had tripled to over 90,000 people. Rathmines and Pembroke townships were the principal developing suburbs whose siren charms lured the fleeing middle classes. What these offered was a well-ordered, genteel environment, well away from the festering slums of the city, as well as an escape from the perceived unresponsive and high-taxing Corporation.

The largest township, Rathmines, came about as development extended southwards beyond the Grand Canal. Those in the forefront – builders, developers and landowners – were frustrated by the lack of facilities that would foster development, such as lighting, water and drainage. Developer and businessman Frederick Stokes was a principal figure in the promotion of the township concept. Public meetings were held: a powerful subtext was the concept of keeping Dublin Corporation at arm's length. It was perceived as inefficient and wasteful of money and of course, was now being run by the ascendant nationalists and liberals.

Influential members of Dublin society who lived in the area added their support, and by 1847, legislation establishing the Rathmines Township was in

Right and below. The most iconic symbol of all the townships: the clock-tower of the Rathmines Town Hall, all red brick and Dumfries red sandstone. The building, which opened in 1897, replaced the earlier town hall. Its verticality was dictated by the need to squeeze the building onto a small footprint – the floor area of a former house.

The Dublin Builder rhapsodised in 1859 that 'villas, single and semi-detached, terraces etc are springing up with an almost fairy-like rapidity' in Rathmines Township. The township came into being in 1847. As well as Rathmines, its area included Rathgar, Ranelagh and Harold's Cross.

Left. One-storey over basement villa in Rathgar.

Left. Detail outside house in Rathmines.

Below left. Pediment at front of house, Rathgar, decorated with gryphon.

Below. In Rathgar, a prominent villa, in unpainted stucco. In true Victorian style, the basement is set mostly above ground level.

place.
The

Above. Large two-storey over basement late-Victorian house in Rathgar. Note the later style of cast and wrought-iron railings.

Right. Clockwise from top far right: Romanesque entrance with polychrome brick details; cast-iron window decoration; Victorian door entrance, still with resonances of the Georgian classical style.

Left. Kenilworth Square, Rathgar. A lion stands guard over this red-brick terrace, with bay windows and stucco door entrances in classical style.

Below left. Upper Beech-wood Avenue, Ranelagh. These houses, which date from the 1870s, originally catered for the clerical classes. One storey high at the front, the front stairs rise up to give these houses a grand entrance.

Below. Rathmines Township became Rathmines Urban District Council in 1899. Lamppost base near Palmerston Park inscribed with its title.

Right. Corbelling (brick projecting from the wall) at the entrance of this red-brick hymn to Victorian elegance in Rathgar. Note the modestly pointed Venetian arch over the doorway.

Below. The nineteenth-century stucco of Bessborough Parade, as it curves towards the Church of Mary Immaculate in Rathmines.

population amounted to around 10,000 at its inception. The township board was dominated by developers, architects, builders and merchants. Like-minded men of property were co-opted as members when vacancies occurred. Rates, or domestic property taxation, were deliberately held at a low level (much lower than those of the dreaded Dublin Corporation over the canal to the north) in order to stimulate growth. The Rathmines Township included Rathmines, Mount Pleasant and Ranelagh, and soon extended to Rathgar and Harold's Cross. In 1859, the *Dublin Builder* rhapsodised about the improvements in Rathmines and Rathgar where 'villas, single and semi-detached, terraces etc. are springing up with an almost fairy-like rapidity, and the green sward speedily gives way to macadamised roads and populous thoroughfares.'

One of the reasons given for founding the township was the poor state of roads. Roads are expensive to pave and maintain. The policy of keeping rates low in Rathmines resulted in unpaved roads in many areas being covered in mud in winter and in dust in summer. Raised crossing points, which facilitated ladies in their long dresses, were placed strategically. The later advent of the tramways, which were obliged to pave around the tram tracks, was a godsend to the townships. Public services such as sanitation and refuse collection were kept to a minimum.

In many cases, the exterior of Victorian houses in Dublin presented a classical, almost plain frontage. The personality of the house tended to be manifested in sometimes elaborate detailing on or around the door in a bewildering array of permutations. Some examples can be seen in this chapter, including the two relatively restrained examples to the left.

Far left. In classical style, a typical Victorian door in Ranelagh.

Near left. Rathgar: cast-iron detailing in the door with a polychrome brick line over the doorway.

Left. Elegant villa in Rathgar, in simple classical style and fine cast-iron detail on the first floor above the entrance.

Above. Window of late-Victorian house in Rathmines. The use of stained glass in houses became increasingly popular as the nineteenth century progressed.

Right. Early nineteenth-century stucco in Rathmines, with fine cast-iron portico.

Right. Muddy roads made doorscrapers essential in the Victorian suburbs.

Below. The importance of fresh air was recognised by the Victorians. Palmerston Park was a late Victorian addition to the Rathmines Township.

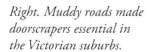
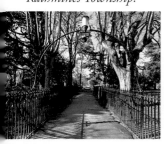

Left. Decorative cast-iron pieces frame this view of the intake bridge at Vartry Reservoir, near Roundwood, County Wicklow. A major advance for public health in the city, Dublin Corporation's Vartry Water Scheme was completed in 1871 and brought a secure potable water supply to Dublin.

Right. Truly heroic engineering through rugged terrain, a pipe bridge over the Dargle River. The supply ran from Vartry Reservoir near Roundwood in Co. Wicklow to Dublin, through a four-kilometre tunnel, thence by a 840-millimetre diameter cast-iron pipe carried over rivers by Gothic-style bridges.

Far left. The valve room at Vartry Reservoir.

Near left. Cast-iron sea horses at the gateway of the entrance to Vartry Lodge, the superintendant's house at the Vartry Reservoir, an elegant Gothic-style residence.

Right. The octagonal, granite Screen House at Stillorgan Reservoir, the Dublin terminus of the Vartry scheme.

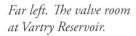

Above. Original control valves at Bohernabreena.

Left. At the reservoir in Vartry, bust of the father of the Vartry Water Scheme, Sir John Gray.

Below left. Rathmines Township declined to join the Vartry Water Scheme. In 1888, it completed its own reservoirs at Boh-ernabreena, Co. Dublin.

Below. 'Rathmines will drain alone.' Drainage pumping station at Lon-donbridge Road in Sandymount.

The issue of water supply became a dominant one. It was sparked by Rathmines Township's obsessions: keeping costs to a minimum and remaining free from the tentacles of Dublin Corporation. Given the realisation that a proper water supply would result in a great increase in public health and prevent such epidemics as cholera, Dublin Corporation began the ambitious Vartry Water Scheme, located near Roundwood in Wicklow, in the 1860s. Rathmines Township was invited to participate, but when they realised that it meant the Corporation laying pipes to houses in the district and charging householders directly, they balked at the idea. Instead, an agreement was reached with the Grand Canal Company for a water supply for Rathmines. Filter beds and a reservoir, situated at the eighth lock on the canal, were completed in 1863. However, problems were encountered in supplying the high ground of the new district of Rathgar. The quality of water originating from the canal proved dubious and there were frequent complaints. Meanwhile, the Corporation's Vartry Water Scheme was completed in 1871. The deficiencies of the canal scheme were apparent in comparison with the pure Wicklow mountain water. The editor of the *Freeman's Journal* reminded readers that, previously, 'the blessings of pure water' had been on offer to Rathmines. Eventually the township commissioners bowed to increasing pressure. After many deliberations, the Bohernabreena upper reservoir, which drained Glenasmole Valley, was constructed and the first water flowed to Rathmines in March 1888.

Sanitary waste disposal, with cesspools and open sewers commonplace and a malodorous Liffey, was primitive in the city for much of the nineteenth century. Improvements in the health of the residents were the motive for Dublin Corporation to develop, in the 1870s, a proposal for a main drainage scheme, with the participation of the surrounding townships. Alas, other townships demurred and Rathmines declared independence once again. Led by the developer Frederick Stokes, chairman of the township board, it refused to be associated with the scheme, fearing higher costs. The board announced that Rathmines 'will drain alone.' After the non-cooperation from the townships, it was to take until 1896 before construction of the Corporation main drainage scheme began. Rathmines and Pembroke townships did cooperate and, in the late 1870s, a drainage scheme was laid down to an outfall near the Pigeon House Fort. Sewage is sewage, no matter what its genteel origin, and the Corporation complained about the material that was subsequently washed onto the shoreline at Merrion.

In the event, the formula of measured expenditure and low rates adopted in Rathmines was successful and new affluent residents were attracted. The population quadrupled in size to 38,000 in 1911. Up to the 1860s and 1870s, housing development catered mainly for the professional classes. Houses were relatively large and imposing. From the 1870s onwards the main trend was in the development of housing for the lower middle classes. The houses built for this market were smaller, terraced and with less decoration than those in the more affluent areas.

There was substantial growth in the other suburbs, albeit not as rapid as in Rathmines. The Fitzwilliam Estate (later the Pembroke Estate) had spread to the south of the Grand Canal in the 1820s. By 1837, large swathes of terraces had been completed on Pembroke Road. Development of Waterloo Road continued

Left. Eagles and lions were suitably martial symbols. These were the favourite statuary for adorning one's villa in the nineteenth century. Other figures sometimes featured like the cockerel at the top, from Ballsbridge and, at bottom right, a sphinx at the entrance to a Victorian terrace in Clontarf.

Right. The former Pembroke Town Hall at Ballsbridge, all Gothic grey stone and red-brick polychromism. The Pembroke Township insisted on high standards being set for the houses that were built in the area.

Right. House in Ballsbridge with red brick polychromism and elaborate cast-iron handrailings. This area was part of the Pembroke Township.

Left. Large house in the Sydney Parade area with tower, topped by cast-iron detail and a turret.

Right. Two doorways in Ballsbridge: polychrome red-brick decoration was popular in this part of the former Pembroke Township.

Below far left. Verandas in the Sydney Parade area. Verandas brought a resonance of the Raj in India.

Below near left. Greek key design on stucco entrance pillar.

Mid right. Simple, but elegant cast iron detail at window, Clyde Road.

Below right. Carved stone classical architrave, with Corinthian capitals and pink granite columns at house in Ballsbridge.

Below. A turret graces this house in Sandymount.

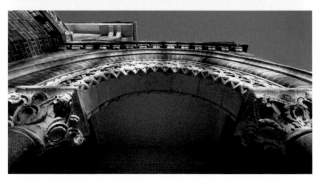

Further examples of decorative door surrounds expressing the personality of classical red-brick house exteriors:

Far left. Two Corinthian columns at either side of this doorway on Clyde Road.

Near left. On Elgin Road, classic and polychrome door entrance. Elaborate cast-iron detail at either side of the door.

Left. Tiles at front of house on Northumberland Road. The scenes are from Sir Walter Scott's novels which were very popular in Victorian times. The scenes depicted here are from: 'Bride of Lammermoor', 'Rob Roy' and 'Heart of Midlothian.'

Left. Floor detail at entrance of the former Masonic Girls' School in Ballsbridge, now Bewley's Hotel.

*Right. As technology de-
veloped, allowing mass-
production, encaustic tiles
became popular during
the Victorian era. Top
and middle: Freemasons'
Hall, Molesworth Street.
Below: St. Patrick's
Cathedral.*

in the 1840s. The 1850s onwards saw development of the area around Raglan and Elgin Roads. The Pembroke Township was created in 1863, at the request of residents. This ranged from Pembroke Road through Sandymount and Ringsend to Irishtown. The Earl of Pembroke owned nearly 80% of the township area. This large, aristocratic land-holding resulted in an air of benevolent paternalism concerning development in Pembroke. The speculator-oriented *laissez-faire* approach in Rathmines did not apply here. Plots were made available to builders, who had to build to a strict specification. Elevations of proposed houses were vetted to see if they were acceptable.

In comparison with the middle-class houses that were being built, Pembroke Township also included what were then hovels in Irishtown and Ringsend. These coexisted uneasily within the township. There was a certain amount of building in the area by employers of artisan cottages for their workers – such as those built by the Dublin South Eastern Railway Company. The township eventually built a few artisan dwellings in Ringsend in the last decade of the nineteenth century. Unlike Rathmines, Pembroke did not provide for the lower middle class and growth in the township declined from the 1880s onwards. The township benefitted from the Pembroke Estate's benevolence: it contributed towards infrastructure and made donations of benefits such as lands, a school and a town hall. Reflecting, perhaps, its more affluent residents, the rates were higher in Pembroke. It was wealthy enough (and not so antagonistic to Dublin Corporation) to embrace the Vartry Water Scheme from its commencement.

Blackrock and Kingstown, further south of Pembroke, originally fishing villages, had developed into seaside resorts at the start of the Victorian era. The visiting Dubliners, on the way to bathe, had many public houses to distract them in Blackrock. The community was mixed: it included such aristocratic landowners as Lord Cloncurry (who had driven a hard bargain to allow the coastal railway along his lands in 1834) and merchants and publicans. The village and surrounding area became a township in 1860.

The nineteenth century brought momentous changes to Kingstown. It had changed its name from Dunleary on the occasion of King George IV's departure in 1821 from its great new harbour. Ireland's first railway, the Dublin and

Above. A train emerges from Dalkey tunnel, with Sorrento Terrace to the right, all multistoreyed stucco, looking over Killiney Bay. The seaside resorts of Kingstown (now Dún Laoghaire), Dalkey and Killiney grew during the Victorian era, thanks to the building of the railway from Dublin along the coast to the south.

Right. Reflecting its confident opulence, the Kingstown Township (now Dún Laoghaire) built its town hall in Venetian style. Construction began in 1878, to a design by J. L. Robinson. To the right is the cast-iron Victoria Fountain. This replica replaces the original which was destroyed in 1982.

Right. Terrace in stucco at Crosthwaite Park in Dún Laoghaire.

Kingstown, which opened in December 1834, connected the well-developed town and its harbour to the city. Emboldened by this great advance, the burghers of Kingstown had declared a township in the year of the opening of the railway. The port and the railway were sources of employment. There was significant housing development within reach of the railway. Population growth was rapid up to the middle of the nineteenth century, although this diminished during its last decades. Dalkey at the start of the century had been a tiny fishing village. It grew after the building of Kingstown harbour, using granite hewn from the Dalkey quarries. The railway southwards to Dalkey (originally served by the innovative atmospheric system which ran from Kingstown from 1844) spurred development there. The townships of Dalkey and adjacent Killiney came into being in the 1860s.

Elsewhere, the railway did not spur suburban development as much as did the horse-tram service. The Bentley Estate (whose principal was a prominent Rathmines developer, Mark Bentley) built houses in what was then the rural Foxrock district, commencing in the 1860s. These were close to Carrickmines and Stillorgan stations on the railway line, which terminated at Harcourt Street. Later, the developers provided land to the railway to build Foxrock station. However, despite large expenditure, growth was slow during the latter half of the nineteenth century.

The northern suburbs began to grow only later in the nineteenth century. In 1859, the *Dublin Builder* noted that 'while the southern suburbs of Dublin are rapidly spreading there is a retrograde movement in the northern'. One constraint to growth in the north of the city up to 1858, when the turnpike system was abolished, was the toll levied on roads heading north from Dublin. Roads to the south did not have to endure such a burden at that time. The sea frontage of Clontarf comprised of low-lying sloblands, which were not perceived as being healthy. This perception was not helped by a proposal in 1865 by a private company to solve Dublin's drainage predicament by depositing sewage in the low-lying area at the Clontarf shore and flooding it. Not surprisingly this scheme did not proceed due to the immediate outcry. The area was under the infuence of the Vernon and Guinness estates. When the township was established after an Act of 1869, the landowner John Vernon was appointed chairman for life. Growth was sluggish until the end of the Victorian era. Throughout its existence the township was short of money and lacked basic amenities. Eventually it was absorbed by Dublin Corporation in 1900.

Another township which was absorbed by the Corporation in 1900 was Drumcondra. It had a short life, being established in 1878. Development grew at a rapid pace here from the 1870s onwards. J. Lombard, a director of Arnotts and E. McMahon, a Home Rule MP, were the two principal developers. Drumcondra's advantage was that it was close to the city centre. It was near enough for people to walk to the centre and avoid the expensive tram fares. Most of the housing catered for the clerical and artisan classes. There were large Catholic educational establishments in the district like the newly-established All Hallows and Clonliffe Colleges. Cardinal Cullen was a strong supporter of the proposal to establish this township.

Kilmainham, which included the Inchicore district, became a township in 1868. It was dominated by institutions and industry. Housing was mostly for

Near right. Red brick was also used in coastal locations near Dublin. Gothic-style arch entrance of house in Monkstown.

Far right and below right. Examples of stucco frontages in Monkstown and Dún Laoghaire.

Below. Stucco facade at Belgrave Square in Monkstown. Stucco was much favoured in seaside locations as it was seen as resisting the penetration of damp.

Left. Facing the sea, Brighton Vale in Monkstown is comprised of single-storey over basement suburban houses. With fine stucco frontage, bay windows and cast-iron detailing, it presents among the best in Victorian maritime architecture in the Dublin area.

Above. Fine cornices and arch in this Ranelagh house. Note the stained-glass roof light. It may also be possible to discern the egg and dart pattern on the cornices, with its classical allusions.

Below. Plaster decorations in the Victorian period were usually factory-made. Public rooms were highly decorated as opposed to the more private rooms such as bedrooms. The cornices of this high-ceilinged room add distinction to this house in Rathgar which dates from 1863. Again, note the egg and dart pattern at the bottom of the cornices.

the working class. A lot of employment was provided by large institutions: there was the gaol, Richmond Barracks, an orphanage and mills. Inchicore village was on the main mail-coach roads to the south. The connection with transport continued with the large Great Southern & Western Railway Works where operations began in 1846. As the works grew this centre of nineteenth-century engineering excellence became a world of its own. It provided a substantial zone of housing around the works for the railway workers. A model school was opened outside the gates in 1853. Kilmainham was predominantly working class and there was a significant Protestant population – over 30% in 1871. This probably reflected the more skilled level of work available on the railway (some had come from Britain with railway experience) as well as the presence of prison warders and soldiers in the population.

The development and dispersal of population in Victorian Dublin's other suburbs had strong religious undertones. The more affluent districts such as the Monkstown area, Rathmines and Pembroke had high Protestant populations. Rathmines had a 46% Protestant population in 1871. The lower middle and working-class sections in the city and townships were predominantly Catholic. This religious and social divide, as we have seen, affected the development of the city as a whole. Each area passed ordinances and took decisions to suit its ruling faction. Dublin Corporation had legislation that benefited nationalist publicans. Rathmines had laws congenial to speculative builders. There was little cooperation on water supply and drainage which could have proved mutually beneficial. The affluent suburbs bitterly opposed annexation by Dublin Corporation. Attacking an 1898 Bill to extend the city boundaries, Sir Edward Carson described Dublin Corporation as 'a sort of Greenwich Hospital for Nationalist wrecks.' This antagonism and lack of direction contributed to Dublin's relatively slow growth in comparison with other cities such as Belfast or Birmingham.

And so the character of residential Dublin in the Victorian ring outside the canals took shape. With the exception of Clontarf, the north side of the city mainly catered for the clerical, artisan and working classes. The affluent generally moved south of the Liffey. There were exceptions to this and, of course, there were the existing working-class areas to the south, such as Ringsend and Irishtown. But the stamp of Victorian social stratification is still fully imprinted on the heart of Dublin, albeit with some exceptions. For example, parts of the central Rathmines area declined into a seedy flatland, which still has not recovered. On the other hand, Portobello and similar artisan areas have been gentrified.

Victoria's reign was so long that there was a significant shift in house style over that time in Dublin. The early style of house is essentially a continuation of Georgian classical. The houses dating from the late 1830s onwards are broadly similar to those of Mountjoy Square and Fitzwilliam Square. The building industry was generally a conservative one, slow to change its techniques and styles, and the classical style was to continue throughout the nineteenth century. However, the Victorian middle classes had less money to spend than the aristocracy who had lived in the wide Georgian squares. Three, two and one storey over basement buildings were the usual styles of speculative housing catering for the middle classes. Terraced or semi-detached, these Victorian

Far left. Victorian doors at Castle Avenue in Clontarf. Clontarf developed later than the townships south of the Liffey. When the horse-tram service was extended there in 1873 it fostered the growth of the township.

Near left. Ornamental entrance to Clontarf Castle, dating from 1885. The castle lands had been owned by the Vernon family since Cromwellian times. The present castle dates from 1837 to a design by William Vitruvius Morrison. The Vernons were leading promoters of development in the Clontarf Township.

houses give the suburban streets an elegance that, sadly, is a rarity in the rest of modern Dublin. In Pembroke, the strict building specifications led to a harmony in the streetscape. Even in the harsher speculative world of Rathmines, the squares and streets generally blended harmoniously together.

The relatively smaller houses of the Victorian middle class are also simpler than the Georgian ones. The typical house would have outer walls built from calp (a dark limestone from quarries in the Dublin region) or granite rubble, clad with brick. The brick colour is predominantly a shade of red. The radical improvements in transport meant that heavy building materials could be sourced from far away. Bricks were now cheap. These had become standardised, machine-made, and, in mid-century, excise duty on bricks was abolished. Bricks came from Irish brickfields, and sometimes from Britain. Local brickworks included Portmarnock, Mount Argus, Bray and Kingstown, with Dolphin's Barn and Clonsilla producing a yellow variety. Georgian houses had been large, but the basement was a relatively hidden feature of the elevation. In Victorian times the basement rose up out of the ground and in many cases became a fully visible part of the elevation of the house. The original Victorian front doors, if intact, can be a joy to behold. These, normally of pitch pine, are above the basement level and reached by imposing stone steps, mostly made from local granite. There can be some decoration at the sides of the door. The fanlight over the door is the classical semi-circle. In the early part of the nineteenth century the fanlight was intersected by a tracery of decorative glazing-bars. Later on, with better glass-making techniques (and importantly, with the abolition of tax on glass and windows by the mid-century), single panes of glass were used. On the main sash windows of the house there was a similar result: larger panes of glass were used from the mid-Victorian period onwards. The type of glazing used is a good indication of the age of the Victorian house.

Another indicator of age is the type of railing. Georgian railings were simple and restrained in style. For most of the Victorian era ironwork became more

Below. Polychrome arch detail with honey-coloured terracotta keystone, from a terraced house at North Strand in Fairview.

Above. A life of Upstairs, Downstairs: bell-pull in the bedroom of a Victorian house in Rathgar. This allowed the lady of the house to call for a servant from the basement where an array of bells was located. Servants were a feature of middle-class life in the Victorian era. In the mid-nineteenth century, if your income was around £200 a year, you could afford a resident maid at £9 a year.

ornate and intricate, albeit of standardised manufacture and pattern. Superbly decorated cast and wrought iron was employed for railings by the footpath and at the side of the front steps. Towards the end of the nineteenth century, this had changed. Square-section rolled wrought iron (steel was used by the turn of the century) was twisted and curved for the railings of the late-Victorian house. These machine-turned railings, alas, lack the charm of the older kind. Given that, in Britain, ironwork such as old railings was taken *en masse* to be smelted down during the Second World War, we are fortunate to have more or less intact a wealth of Victorian ironwork, from the early through to the late period, still extant in the Dublin suburbs of that era.

Exploring a suburban house of the middle rank, one enters the front door into a hallway that is large by today's standards. The ceilings are high. Elegance and classical proportion were the main reasons for this, as opposed to minor considerations like the difficulty of heating a house. The Victorians embellished the more public areas, as opposed to private rooms like bedrooms which had plain ornamentation. Thus, decorative plaster cornices were usually found on the edge of ceilings in the rooms on the hall floor. Adjacent to the hallway there is a large living room and a dining room. These each have a fireplace, as do the bedrooms. With elaborate decoration, materials such as marble with cast iron have been used for the fire surround. A pair of large doors, which can be folded back, interconnects the living and dining rooms. Upstairs are the bedrooms; downstairs in the basement are the kitchen, scullery and the servants' quarters. The servants could be called by a bell system which rang in the kitchen. Servants were necessary for the aspiring middle classes. In *The Victorian House*, the authors Marshall and Wilcox tell of the financial dynamic necessary to 'arrive': 'In 1840 it was estimated that you needed a minimum salary of £150 a year to keep a servant; out of that salary you would pay £3 a year for a servant to come in and clean. At £200 per annum you could afford a resident maid at £9 a year, and if you could clear £250 a year you had arrived and your wife became a "lady".'

From the 1870s onwards, most housing developments catered for the middle to lower strata of the social spectrum. The Victorian sense of propriety and decorum ensured that one's status in life was reflected by the ornamentation on one's house. Many of the houses for the lower middle class were terraced red-brick with relatively limited ornamentation, even in the more public areas of the house. The houses at Upper Beechwood Avenue, Ranelagh, are a magnificent example of smaller houses, which catered for the clerical classes, and did successfully achieve balance and elegance. The concept of a flight of stairs to the front door is continued in these terraced houses. Even though the main floor is raised a metre or so over footpath level, the basement now has lost its importance. It is small and in some of the houses it has not been developed: there is just a cavity filled with earth. Upstairs are the bedrooms. These houses copy, on a smaller scale, the ornamentation of the larger house: decorative plaster cornices and fine fireplaces.

New housing for the working class came to the fore only later in the nineteenth century. Throughout that century, the poorer people, living in the old, crowded districts such as the Liberties, had managed to improve their lot somewhat by a gradual migration to the vacant large houses (which became

Left. Great Western Square near Broadstone Station. These red-brick two-storey houses were provided by the Midland Great Western Railway for its workers.

Left. At Gray Street in the Liberties. Towards the end of the Victorian era, the Dublin Artisans' Dwelling Company built houses in the area.

Above. With a Gothic-style entrance, substantial terraced houses in Inchicore, near the Railway Works there. The Great Southern & Western Railway built a large number of houses, of different sizes, for their employees.

Right. Terraced houses provided for employees at Portrane Asylum (now St. Ita's), where construction commenced in 1896.

tenements) to the north of the Liffey. These houses had remained empty since the flight of the aristocracy and the departure of the middle classes to the new suburbs. Overall, Dublin was a most unhealthy city with one of the highest proportions of poor people in Europe. The death rate amongst the poorer classes was much higher than in comparable cities in Britain.

The plight of those living in the slums was recognised by such bodies as the Dublin Artisans' Dwelling Company, founded in 1876. Its objective was to build houses for the working class at a reasonable cost. Various schemes were constructed in the decades that followed, including such areas as the Coombe and Harold's Cross. Several thousand dwellings were constructed. However, most of the clientele were artisans, who were relatively better off. Dublin Corporation came late to this endeavour. Its first buildings were several four-storeyed blocks at Barrack (now Benburb) Street, completed in 1887. Other townships, reluctantly in some cases, built houses for the working classes. Rathmines's first public housing was in the Gulistan area, behind the present town hall. Cottages were built there, the first group being completed in 1895. Many employers provided houses for their workers. Transport companies were particularly active in this. Reference has been made to the ring of railway workers' houses spread around the Great Southern & Western Railway works at

Above. The problem of providing housing for the less well-off was addressed only late in the nineteenth century. Dublin Corporation's first housing for working people was these four-storeyed blocks (1887) at Barrack (now Benburb) Street.

Left. Rathmines Township's first venture in providing houses for the working class was in 1895 in the Gulistan area, behind the town hall.

Right. Philanthropic housing. With Guinness funding, the Iveagh Trust provided this large complex of housing blocks, near Christ Church Cathedral, where building commenced in the 1890s. The standard of these buildings was very high.

Below. Single-storey terraced houses in Glasnevin, with polychrome brick arches over the doors.

Inchicore. Great Western Square, near Broadstone Station is a fine testament to the solid houses built by the Midland Great Western Railway. Tram workers were accommodated in terraces of small houses near the tram depots all over the city. Lord Iveagh donated money to acquire four acres in the Bull Alley area, clear the slums there and build a group of large blocks of flats. This philanthropic scheme, which began in the last years of the nineteenth century, was managed by the Iveagh Trust and answered the needs of unskilled workers. Care was taken to achieve good ventilation and lighting.

There are many other house styles than the ones described above. Stucco became a generic term for external plasterwork and has properties of resisting wind-blown rain better than bare brickwork. Victorian stucco-fronted houses can be seen all over Dublin. However, the majority are located in areas along the coast. Indeed, it could be called the Dublin maritime villa style. They are to be found in profusion in Blackrock, Monkstown, Dún Laoghaire, Dalkey and along the aristocratic slopes of Killiney. Generally well-kept and well-painted, terraces of this kind of house along the coastal roads provide a pleasant vista along the shores of Dublin Bay.

In the later-Victorian period, the speculative builders became more adventurous, breaking free from the simplicity of the classical style. Perhaps it was as a counterpoint to the self-important, improving ideas and high morality of Victorian society that there came about a surprising nostalgia for medieval art and architecture. The ideas of British architects such as as Pugin (Gothic) and Ruskin (medieval north Italian) were embraced in Ireland and amplified by local architects. This can be seen in Dublin domestic architecture of the mid- to late-Victorian era. Door entrances were designed in the medieval Italian style using a Venetian Gothic arch. This style is particularly to be seen in (what are now) the Dublin 4 areas such as Clyde and Elgin Roads. The same theme was continued by the use of polychromy. This is the use of different textures and colours of building materials to give decoration to buildings. Patterns of various shades of brick were the usual method employed in Dublin houses. This was economical, as well as providing colour against the grey skies of the city. This technique became very popular and was used in all types of house from the modest to the grand. The extensive use of bay windows and corbelled brick would continue into Edwardian times. Terracotta became popular after the 1860s. It was cheaper than equivalent carved-stone decoration. However, its use in Dublin's houses was relatively restrained compared to the exuberant use of terracotta on public and commercial buildings.

From the artisan terraces of Phibsboro to the rather patrician residences of Dublin 4, Victorian houses generally have one pleasing feature: weathered reddish brick. It can be said of Dublin that its sometimes grimy Victorian heart is red. On a clear Autumn or Spring day, it is a quintessentially Dublin scene, to see the sun shining tangentially on the serried rows of red-bricked Victorian houses. Mercifully, these have survived, in the main. Generally, houses have not suffered the same fate as commercial buildings in the centre of the city. We can be grateful that the recent property boom resulted in the destruction of only a limited number of Victorian buildings. The essential Victorian suburb still adorns Dublin, north and south of the Liffey.

Chapter 3
Mind and Soul

Catholic Emancipation in 1829 marked a change of power structures in Ireland. Up to then the establishment was firmly Protestant in Dublin. During the Victorian era, this position gradually eroded as a result of a rise in Catholic influence and power. One manifestation of this change in Dublin was the rapid building of Catholic churches and other buildings. With Catholic nationalism on the ascent, the mainly Protestant middle class retrenched to the suburbs. Sectarian tension was always simmering below the surface in the nineteenth century.

Centuries ago, Dublin was a very small city and distinctly different from the rest of Ireland. A census of 1659 listed over two thirds of the city's population as English, with less than a third as Irish. The eighteenth century brought an enormous growth. It became a centre of wealth and culture, a city of fine avenues and buildings. In addition to a steady trickle of people from Britain, there was a flood of rural migrants, predominantly Catholic, to the city, mostly from surrounding counties. This movement of people, over time, was to radically change the city's social, religious and political complexion. It is estimated that, by the first decades of the nineteenth century, the number of Catholics had grown to around 70% of Dublin's population. Nevertheless, the significant Protestant minority enjoyed an overwhelming command of wealth, power and influence. Members of the Established Church (Church of Ireland) made up the bulk of the Protestant population. Unlike the north-eastern part of Ireland, Dublin was not a Presbyterian stronghold. Presbyterians amounted to only one in ten of the Protestants in the city.

After the Battle of the Boyne in 1690, repression of Catholics was put on a statutory basis by enactment of the Penal Laws in 1695. A century later, the Penal Laws were gradually repealed. Catholic Emancipation in 1829 ended remaining formal restrictions. As we have seen, in Dublin, Catholics were in a majority but wielded little commercial or social power. It could be said that 1829 marked the beginning of the change from a primarily Protestant city to a predominantly Catholic one.

During the early years of the nineteenth century, most of the Catholic population of Dublin was working class. As the century progressed, a rising Catholic middle class concentrated on entering the professions of medicine and law. Elsewhere, the ranks of the lower middle classes were boosted by emergent Catholic publicans and grocers, mainly of rural origin.

Protestants had been among the leaders of the United Irishmen. Now, as the nineteenth century progressed, Protestant republicanism was becoming a distant memory. The tectonic plates had shifted and religious differences were magnified. After Emancipation, Catholics gained membership of Dublin Corporation. As a result the Corporation began to focus more on nationalist issues and less on municipal matters. This added to the alienation of the Protestant middle classes who, for this and other reasons, migrated to the middle-class suburbs to the south of the Grand Canal – all of which added to the polarisation of the religions. The disestablishment of the Church of Ireland by an Act of 1869 added to the sense of insecurity of its members.

The emergence of Catholic power was made manifest in a physical way in the streets of Dublin. As the repression of the penal times faded away, the Catholic Church began building *con brio*. In Dublin work began on the Pro-Cathedral in 1816. Located in the relatively discreet setting of Marlborough Street, this Greek Doric structure is said to be principally modelled on the church of St. Philippe du Roule in Paris. The Franciscan Church of the Immaculate Conception (also known as Adam and Eve's) on Merchants' Quay was commenced in 1834 to a design by Patrick Byrne. Again, the church presents a reserved appearance along the quayside. The main entrance is from a side street at the back. In time the siting and presentation of churches began to improve. The Jesuit St. Francis Xavier's church (1832, J. B. Keane) merges well with the

Right. Called an example of 'heroic post-Emancipation classicism', Patrick Byrne's St. Paul's Church on Arran Quay (1835-44) elegantly proclaims the new religious reality in Dublin.

Below. On high in High Street: St. Audoen's Church, again classical and in a prominent position, is also by Patrick Byrne. It dates from 1846. The portico was added decades later. This was a common practice – the delay was due to lack of funds.

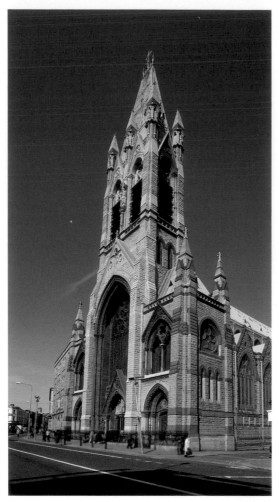

Left. Ascending to heaven: the Augustinian Church of Saints Augustine and John dominates Thomas Street. Construction began in 1862. It took 33 years to complete due to shortage of funds. Fully demonstrating the verticality of A. W. Pugin's intense Gothic style, it was designed by Pugin's son E. W. Pugin and his partner George Ashlin. Ruskin said, on viewing the plans, that it would be a 'poem in stone.'

Left. St. Nicholas of Myra, set back from Francis Street, is a bold example of the classical style, popular immediately after Catholic Emancipation. It dates from 1834 and was designed by John Leeson. The Ionic portico was added two decades later.

Above. The front of Saints Augustine and John was called 'perhaps the noblest and most striking façade of ecclesiastical art in this country.' An arch of angels ascending in this detail of carved red sandstone.

Right. The soaring interior of the Church of Saints Augustine and John.

Right. The magnificent ceiling of St. Nicholas of Myra.
Below. A panel in the ceiling which depicts the coat of arms of the Isle of Man. With links between Manx Catholics and Dublin dating back to the Reformation, the Isle of Man was included in the diocese of Francis Street until 1850.

Georgian streetscape of Upper Gardiner Street. So does St. Andrew's, Westland Row, by James Bolger, which was completed in 1843.

As the century continued, the pace of church-building increased. This asserted the new reality: the Catholic Church had arrived and was no longer the church of the side streets. The new churches were prominent in location, being on a main street or on a height, as well as employing a proclamatory style of architecture. Patrick Byrne designed St. Paul's on Arran Quay (1835-44) which is in sharp contrast to his previous restrained 'Adam and Eve's' of some years before. Christine Casey, in *Dublin* calls it an example of 'heroic post-Emancipation classicism.' Not far from the Four Courts, it sits elegantly on the quayside. The Greek Ionic portico casts a pleasing reflection on the waters of the river Liffey. Another of Byrne's churches is in a dominant position overlooking the river. St. Audoen's was dedicated in 1846, and fronts onto the appropriately-named High Street. The impressive portico, however, is a later addition, dating from 1899. Not far away is the church of St. Nicholas of Myra, which was designed by John Leeson and dates from 1834. Uncharacteristically, this is set back from Francis Street. However, it does have the usual imposing classical façade, this time an Ionic portico (added over two decades later).

The Famine slowed the pace of building, which, however, recommenced during the second half of the nineteenth century: new churches, monasteries, convents and seminaries were built all over the city. In a change from classicism, Gothic architecture became the fashion for new ecclesiastical buildings. Patrick

Above. The church of St. Saviour in Dominick Street, all pointed arches and neo-Gothicism. It was designed by J. J. McCarthy, who was known as the 'Irish Pugin.' It dates from 1861.

Above. Another work by J. J. McCarthy, this time in the Romanesque style. The Passionist Church of St. Paul of the Cross, at Mount Argus, was completed in 1878. McCarthy benefited from the post-Emancipation surge in church building and secured many commissions for Irish Catholic churches.

Byrne used this style for his St. James's Church (on James's Street), which was completed in 1859. The architect J. B. Keane designed the Gothic St. Lawrence O'Toole Church on Seville Place, which he began in 1844.

By the mid-nineteenth century, the architectural world was a ferment of competing theories on the appropriate architectural style. In the midst of Victorian affluence, many styles were under consideration including Gothic, Elizabethan, and through John Ruskin – the medieval architecture of northern Italy. The debate attained a high seriousness. The intense convert to Catholicism, A. W. Pugin (1812-1852) declared that all classical architecture was false. He argued forcefully for the verticality of the Gothic style, with its roots in the Middle Ages. Verticality was all, when he carried out the designs of many Catholic churches in Britain and several buildings in Ireland, including the cathedral at Killarney and St. Patrick's College in Maynooth. Pugin's influence extended to Irish architects, supported not least by the articles he wrote in the *Dublin Review*. J. J. McCarthy (who had worked with Pugin at Maynooth) became known as the 'Irish Pugin'. In addition to many churches around the country he designed the church of St. Saviour on Dominick Street, regarded as his finest. It dates from 1861 and, with its pointed arches and delicate carving, is in true neo-Gothic style. The Pugin tradition continued with the church of Saints Augustine and John in Thomas Street. This Augustinian church was begun in 1862, designed by Pugin's son E. W. Pugin and his partner George Ashlin. The story goes that when Ruskin looked at the designs he said that it would be a

Left. A Byzantine jewel in the heart of the city. The University Church on St. Stephen's Green was established by John Henry (later Cardinal, now Saint) Newman. It opened in 1856 to a design by John Hungerford Pollen.

Right. The interior is modelled on a Roman basilica. Amidst the contemporary dominance of classical and Gothic-style churches in Dublin, it represented a refreshing change.

Below. Bust of John Henry Newman (1801-1890) in the University Church.

Ecclesiastical stone carving: Top right, detail on eaves of Christ Church Cathedral. Middle right, entrance to monumental chapel at Glasnevin Cemetery. Below right, entrance to St. Patrick's Cathedral.

Left. In serried ranks, the soldiers of Victoria: the gravestones of soldiers who served in nineteenth-century Dublin are stacked along the eastern wall of the former garrison cemetery at Arbour Hill.

Left. Described by Christine Casey in her book on Dublin as 'a curiously eclectic building of gauche charm', the church of the Sacred Heart at Arbour Hill was originally the chapel of the military prison, and dates from 1850.

Below far left. The Catholic church of Mary Immaculate in Rathmines was designed by Patrick Byrne in his usual classical style (1854). He also designed the Church of the Three Patrons (near left), in Rathgar, which dates from 1860. This has one of the plainest facades of any Dublin church and still awaits its planned portico. Local sectarian hackles were raised when each church was built.

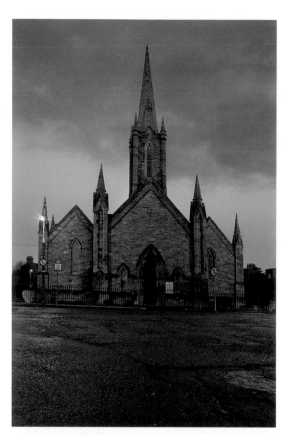

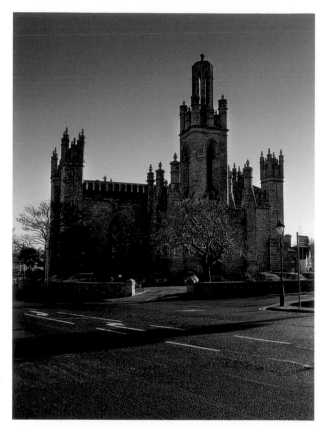

John Semple's spires rise to the heavens:

Far left. Semple's Gothic Holy Trinity Church in Rathmines is elegant in its clear verticality, and dates from 1833.

Near left. Semple's masterpiece: the Church of Ireland Monkstown Church, dating from 1831, unusual both externally and internally. The Gothic castellations are like pieces on a chessboard. It is said that this was John Betjeman's favourite church.

The interior of Monkstown Church, right and below left, is an exuberant and eccentric exercise in decorative plasterwork. It is one of the most flamboyant interiors of any nineteenth-century building in the Dublin area.

Below. The grey granite entrance of Monkstown Church.

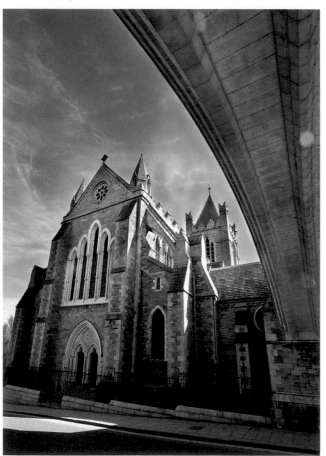

'poem in stone.' Lack of funds meant that the church took 33 years to complete. Located on the heights above the Liffey, its towering Gothic spire is a landmark in the city. Christine Casey in *Dublin* calls it the most original Victorian Gothic church in Dublin.

Most churches built in the Dublin area in the second half of the nineteenth century were of the Gothic style. A refreshingly different style is employed at the University Church on St. Stephen's Green. John Henry Newman (later Cardinal, now Saint) had come to set up a Catholic University in Dublin. It foundered, but before he left in 1859 he was responsible for the establishment of the church, which opened in 1856. Designed by John Hungerford Pollen, it has references to the Roman church of S. Paolo fuori le Mura. It is in a Byzantine style and influenced by Ruskin's *Stones of Venice*. Maurice Craig, in his *Dublin 1660-1860,* calls it a 'delightful building … emphatically re-vival rather than sur-vival'.

Patrick Byrne continued with the classical style when he designed the Church of Mary Immaculate in Rathmines. The church was built in 1854, but the present portico was not completed until 1881. Rathmines was expanding and new villas and terraces were being built for the middle classes. However, all was not well; there was an undercurrent of sectarian tension. This was made manifest when, at the new church on feast-days like Corpus Christi, a screen had to be erected to mask the proceedings and not to offend the sensibilities of the local populace. Byrne also designed the Church of the Three Patrons in Rathgar. One of the reasons for its construction was to make it easier for domestic servants of the locality (most of whom were Catholic) to attend mass. The church has one of the plainest fronts in Dublin. It was intended to construct a portico at a later stage when funds permitted, but this was never done. Sectarianism surfaced, after the ceremony to lay the foundation stone, when the *Irish Times* of the twentieth of March, 1860 thundered: 'On Sunday last, the Protes-

Victorian Dublin had many memorials to Irishmen who participated in the numerous wars fought by the British Empire around the globe.

The Crimean War made a big impact. Top left, plaque on Rathgar Road named after the battle at the Malakoff bastion at Sevastopol. Far left, memorial to a Major-General who participated in the Charge of the Light Brigade, as well as the suppressing of the Indian Mutiny. Near left, memorial to soldiers of the Royal Irish Regiment killed in the Crimea.

Left. Memorial in St. Patrick's Cathedral to the fallen of the Royal Irish Regiment in the China War (1839-42). Lieutenant-Colonel Tomlinson expires heroically at the Battle of Chapoo. The conflict was known as the Opium War and arose from China's attempt to stamp out the opium trade. Britain won and gained concessions, including the territory of Hong Kong, from the Chinese.

Left. Also in St. Patrick's, memorial to the fallen of the Royal Irish Regiment in the Burma War (1852-3). Scene from the storming of the Shoe Dagon Pagoda, Rangoon. The British occupied lower Burma as a consequence of the war.

Above. The Royal Irish Regiment had an eventful nineteenth century. Another memorial to members of the regiment who fell in Crimea (1855-56), in stained glass, at St. Patrick's Cathedral.

Clockwise from top right, memorials to conflict: Sudan, 1885; conflicts in India, including the Mutiny; India again with Lieutenant Smith, late of Mountjoy Square and killed at the battle of Hyderabad in 1843; Lieutenant-General Havelock fought in the Persian and Indian Mutiny campaigns as well as the New Zealand War (1863-65) and was killed by Afridis in the Khyber Pass in 1897; an Irish wolfhound guards a war memorial.

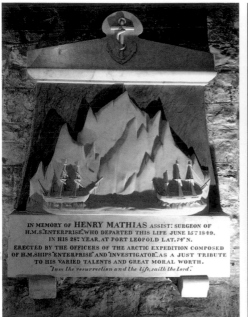

Victorian derring-do and heroism:

Far left. In Christ Church Cathedral, memorial to Dublin-born Henry Mathias who was assistant surgeon during the Arctic voyages of HMS 'Enterprise' and 'Investigator' in 1849. This was one of the expeditions which searched for the ill-fated Franklin expedition.

Near left. In St. Patrick's Cathedral, memorial to John McNeill Boyd, captain of HMS 'Ajax', who was lost off the rocks at Kingstown (now Dún Laoghaire) when attempting to save the crew of the brig 'Neptune'.

Left. Veranda with cast-iron columns adjacent to the Molyneux Home at Leeson Park.

Dissenters built many churches in Dublin during the nineteenth and early twentieth centuries. From left, some examples: the Presbyterian Christ Church in Rathgar, dating from 1865; the central octagon of the former Methodist Church, Dolphin's Barn, completed in 1902; the former Moravian Church at Kevin Street.

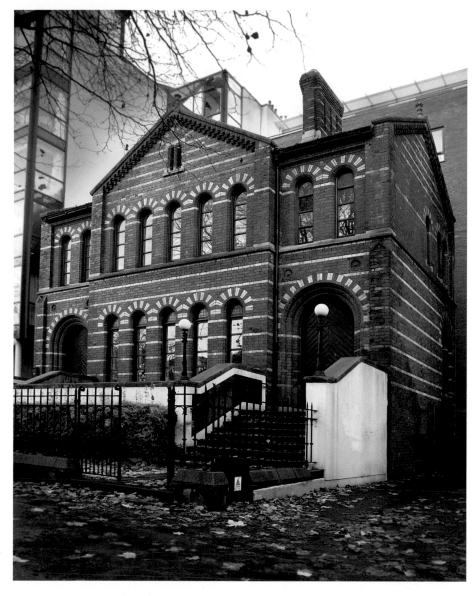

Right. Synagogue at Adelaide Road. J. J. O' Callaghan designed this polychrome red-brick building in 1892. Many Eastern European Jews settled in Dublin during the latter years of the Victorian era.

Below. Polychromism reigns in this brick pattern on the frontage of the Gospel Hall in Upper Rathmines Road. The building dates from 1890 and was formerly the 'Orange and Protestant' Hall.

tant and quiet township of Rathgar was the scene of mob-fanaticism and priestly display. A Chapel, it seems, is to depreciate the value of the property of the neighbourhood, and drive the Protestant occupants from the place.'

Despite its slow decline over the nineteenth century the Established Church continued to build churches. Prominent were St. George's, Hardwicke Place (1813), St. Stephen's, Mount Street Crescent, completed in 1827 (known as the 'Pepper Canister Church') and the 'Black Church' in St. Mary's Place by John Semple, completed in 1830. Semple also designed an unusual church at Monkstown (1831). Constructed in grey granite, the church has an enormous array of Gothic castellations which can only be compared to pieces on a chess board. The interior is magnificent. It presents the most flamboyant church interior of nineteenth-century Dublin. Examples of Church of Ireland construction in the second half of the nineteenth century include St. John the Evangelist,

Left. Early nineteenth-century 'mortsafe' at the graveyard in Drumcondra. This iron enclosure over the grave was to guard against 'resurrectionists' or body-snatchers. With many medical schools, Dublin was a prime location for this trade. Bodies were also exported at £40 each to schools of anatomy in London and Edinburgh.

Far left. One of the castellated watchtowers erected on the perimeter of Glasnevin Cemetery. These served as lookouts for armed night-watchmen, in their struggle against the 'resurrectionists' who plagued the cemetery during its early years.

Near left. Cardinal McCabe's dying request was to be buried simply. This was to no avail as he now rests in this elaborate Hiberno-Romanesque canopied monument in Glasnevin. It dates from 1888, to a design by George Ashlin.

Left. Hands clasped for eternity, captured in cast iron at Glasnevin.

In Victorian Dublin, just because you were dead did not mean you escaped the sectarian divide. As the nineteenth century progressed most Catholics were buried in Glasnevin Cemetery and Protestants in Mount Jerome Cemetery.

Glasnevin Cemetery dates from 1831 when Daniel O'Connell's Catholic Association bought nine acres in the locality.

Right. Entrance to the crypt housing O'Connell's tomb at the cemetery in Glasnevin.

Below right. Eyes to heaven, a statue with a star and anchor in front of the Mortuary Chapel, Glasnevin. Is it Mary as Stella Maris, Star of the Sea? There is a similar statue in Mount Jerome Cemetery.

Below. The monument to O'Connell, over his tomb, is a round tower, the highest in Ireland. It dates from 1861.

Left. Roman classicism is manifest at the tomb of John Philpot Curran at Glasnevin. Designed by George Papworth, it is based on the Roman sacrophagus of the Roman consul Scipio Barbatus, (now in the Vatican Museum).

Right. Classicism was popular also in Mount Jerome Cemetery. The cemetery was consecrated by the Church of Ireland Archbishop of Dublin in 1836.

Left. In Mount Jerome, the Gresham tomb. The lady interred here had a dread of being buried alive. A bell, placed on top of the tomb, was linked by a chain to the coffin. It would have allowed the occupant to call attention in the felicitous event that she awoke. The coffin itself had special spring-loaded locks, allowing quick release from within.

Right. The Harvie memorial, with a faithful dog howling above his master's cloak, at Mount Jerome. His master was drowning and, standing on the cloak, the dog barked to call for help. Later, when it died, the dog was interred here with his master.

The large Victorian memorials of Mount Jerome demonstrate the self-aggrandisement of the rich and powerful, as they pass through the portals to the next life.

Above left. Small but perfectly formed: two Graeco-Roman temples.

Above. In the bowels of the earth, terraced vaults seen on a misty morning.

Above right. A solid cast-iron door guards a vault.

Left. A substantial tomb with fine cast-iron railings which decayed and collapsed over time.

Clyde Road (1867). The Dissenters also continued to build and there is a myriad of their nineteenth-century churches all over the city, ranging from the grandiose to the diminutive. Described as 'large and flamboyant', the Abbey Presbyterian Church of 1864 (known as Findlater's church) sits in harmony at the corner of Parnell Square.

The sectarian divide in Dublin continued even after death. Originally, Catholics and Protestants were buried in Glasnevin Cemetery, but this rapidly changed when Mount Jerome opened (in 1836) and the majority of Protestants were interred there during the nineteenth century. Glasnevin Cemetery had its beginnings in 1831 when Daniel O'Connell's Catholic Association bought nine acres at Glasnevin. In its early years the cemetery suffered from a spate of body-snatching. Bodies were stolen and sold to doctors and students for dissection. Dublin was reputed to be a prime location of this 'trade' in these islands (along with London and Edinburgh), with bodies being exported at £40 each. Watch-towers were set at the corners of the walls that encircled the cemetery, so that a lookout could be kept for body-snatchers, also known as 'resurrectionists'. As late as 1853, a pack of Cuban bloodhounds was on patrol to deter the macabre commerce in bodies.

Funerals were matters of some import in Victorian Dublin. Large crowds attended. Both Glasnevin and Mount Jerome daily received large processions, with carriages pulled by horses crowned with plumes. In his book *Dublin: the*

Left. Stained glass of nineteenth-century Dublin.

Far left. The arms of Albert Edward, Prince of Wales, installed in 1873 as Grand Master of the Religious and Military Order of the Temple for 'all the possessions, colonies and dependencies', in the Freemasons' Hall at Molesworth Street.

Near left. Window (with some broken panes) and cherub in crypt, Glasnevin cemetery.

Far left. 'Charity never faileth', memorial at the Freemasons' Hall. This stained glass was originally located in the Masonic Girls' School at Ballsbridge.

Near left. Pre-Raphaelite figures depicting Music and the Arts, dating from 1894, at 18 Parnell Square (now the Writers' Museum). This was once the residence of George Jameson, of the whiskey distilling family, who remodelled the house in 1891-95. The Jameson family coat of arms is shown in the lower left of the window.

Far left. Michelangelo depicted at the entrance of the National Library, which was completed in 1890.

Near left. Stained-glass window in the bridge connecting the Synod House to Christ Church Cathedral.

The setting up of the National Board of Education in 1831 gave the impetus to development of a national educational system and the building of national schools across Ireland.

Right. Two-storey, red-brick building with prominent corbelling, St. Kevin's Female National Schools on Grantham Street, dating from 1886.

Right. The red brick and limestone of St. Columba's Infant National Schools at North Strand.

Right. Classical and separate, the entrances for boys and girls at this former school on Upper Rathmines Road.

Left. The yellow terracotta and red brick on a gable of the former Dublin Working Boys' Home and Harding Technical School, Lord Edward Street (now a youth hostel, Kinlay House).

Right. On Rathgar Avenue, the Methodist Rathgar National School, dating from 1896.

Left. The Central Model Schools, off Marlborough Street, by F. Darley, dating from 1859 and still used as a National School. Christine Casey, in her book 'Dublin', commented that the design of the building 'has something of an Italianate railway station.'

Left. The former St. Stephen's Schools (now a hotel) at Northumberland Road. Construction commenced in 1859 to a design by Deane and Woodward.

Right. Now St. Michael's Special School, this late-Victorian building at Grosvenor Road, Rathmines is clad in polychrome red brick and with decorative barge boards.

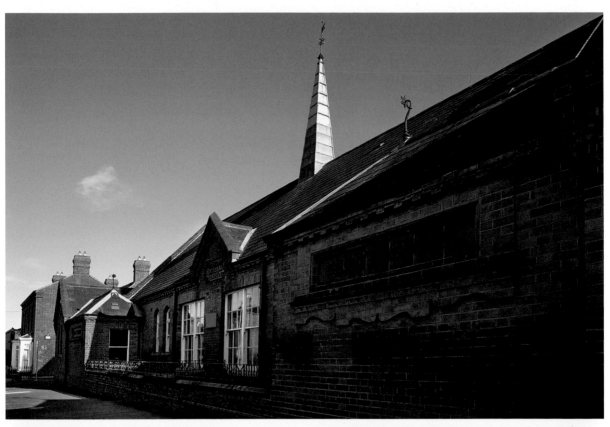

Left. The former St. Andrews National Schools, for boys and girls, in Pearse Street, with terracotta and brick frontage, which dates from 1895. It was designed by William Hague, a prominent church architect.

Left. On Ailesbury Road, Ballsbridge, originally a Victorian villa with tower in Italian Romanesque style, attributed to J. J. McCarthy. It is now St. Michael's School.

Below far left. Red-brick polychromy and terracotta at the the former Dublin Working Boys' Home and Harding Technical School, Lord Edward Street, dating from 1891. Described as 'High Victorian Jacobean' style.

Near left. With a Masonic insignia over the date of 1895, a gable of the Masonic Girls' School, Ballsbridge, now a hotel.

Right. Originally built as a manor house, Mount Temple School in Clontarf. Designed by Lanyon and Lynn (1862) in Gothic Revival style.

Below. Statue of Cardinal Cullen (1803-78) in the Pro-Cathedral, Marlborough Street. Ultramontane, he shaped the Irish Catholic Church of the mid-nineteenth century, then growing in power and influence, into rigid adherence to Papal authority.

Fair City Peter Somerville-Large recounts how a visitor in the 1860s, noting the vast number of horses attending funerals commented '... the animals could find their way to the different cemeteries ... in the dark ...' The Victorians took themselves seriously and their passing was marked by elaborate statuary. It is fitting that the 57-metre high tower that dominates Glasnevin was erected to commemorate O'Connell, the man whose vision led to the establishment of the cemetery. It is pleasant to walk in the older parts of Glasnevin Cemetery. The leaning monuments have recently been straightened and renovated. Here we see the citizens of the last century commemorated on a heroic scale. In 1859 the *Dublin Builder* conceded that 'the monuments are generally of the usual promiscuous character in point of design, but some very beautiful and tasteful structures nevertheless are to be found.' The same journal was not very complimentary about Mount Jerome Cemetery. It said 'An equivalent amount of taste has not been bestowed here on the landscaping of the grounds, as at Glasnevin.' Despite that rather acerbic view, Mount Jerome presents a wonderful Victorian funerary style. Here the mausoleums, vaults and statuary are large and of some substance, for here were buried the *haute bourgeoisie* of Dublin. The older part of the cemetery is clustered with graves of Victorian merchant princes, professional men, scholars, soldiers and artists. There are several large and impressive neo-classical monuments. One poignant statue is that of a dog howling to the heavens, mourning his lost master. Notable Victorians buried here include Sir William Wilde, Thomas Davis, Sheridan Le Fanu and William Rowan Hamilton.

The Catholic Archbishop of Dublin, Paul Cullen, was appointed in 1852. He became Ireland's first Cardinal in 1866. Previously Rector of the Irish College in Rome, he was a strong disciplinarian. He is regarded as being of the ultramontane tradition, in which Papal authority was asserted over the local clergy. He ensured that a more regulated approach was taken in the Irish Church, which hitherto had a tendency to go its own way. He encouraged the development of a Catholic secondary school system run by religious orders. The Chris-

Above. Detail from the O'Brien Institute.

Near left. The former O'Brien Institute in Marino was a charitable orphanage dating from 1881. It makes a striking red Gothic contrast to the pure classicism of the nearby eighteenth-century Casino.

Far left. The former College of Education at Carysfort, Blackrock (now the Smurfit School of Business) was founded in 1877.

Right. The campanile at Trinity College Dublin, by Sir Charles Lanyon dating from 1853.

Left. All Hallows College was founded in 1842 as a missionary seminary. Large and imposing, it is a symbol of the rapid growth in the numbers of the Catholic clergy that took place in the nineteenth century. These buildings date from around the mid-century.

Right. Detail and view of the Graduates' Memorial Building, Trinity College, by Thomas Drew, which dates from 1899.

Left. One of the finest Victorian buildings in Dublin: the Museum Building in Trinity College, by Sir Thomas Deane and Benjamin Woodward, dating from 1853-57. It brings, with exuberance, the romance of medieval Venice to central Dublin. It was a precursor to the partnership's acclaimed Oxford Museum of Natural History. The stone carvers, the O'Shea brothers, who worked here in Trinity also worked on the Oxford building.

Right. Echoes of Byzantium, two domes crown the magnificent entrance hall of the Museum Building.

Left. A view of the Museum Building. Contrast this with, below, a view of the Great Mosque of Córdoba, from al-Andalus of the tenth century which was influenced by the polychrome arches of ancient Rome and its successor, Byzantium. Venetian architecture was also influenced by Byzantium. Deane and Woodward's work here reflects the Victorian enthusiasm for the Venetian style.

tian Brothers catered for the humbler end of the social scale. The aspirations of the rising Catholic middle class were served by such colleges as Blackrock and Terenure (both dating from 1860). The overall take-up of education by Catholics, while rising, was a gradual one. For example, in 1891, 1.2% of Catholics were receiving secondary education, in comparison with 6.5% of members of the Church of Ireland.

In the early years of the nineteenth century the state had paid a grant to the Kildare Place Society with the intention of supporting non-denominational education. Suspicions of proselytizing arose, which led, in 1831, to the transfer of the grant to a new government board, the National Board of Education, on which representatives of the three main denominations sat. The purpose was to set up a national system of education. It provided grants for teachers' salaries, for textbooks and towards school building costs. In the underlying sectarian atmosphere of nineteenth-century Ireland, the original wish for 'mixed' education did not materialise. By 1900, while literacy had radically improved among the population, most 'national' schools were denominational.

The Queen's University was set up, based on the Colleges (Ireland) Act of 1845. There were three colleges, in Cork, Belfast and Galway. This university was intended by the Government to provide a non-denominational alternative to Trinity College, Dublin (at that time larger than Oxford University), then predominantly catering for Established Church members. There was immediate opposition from the Catholic bishops and clergy, with Archbishop Cullen in full voice. Daniel O'Connell called them 'godless colleges.' As a reaction to this, in 1854 the Catholic hierarchy established in Dublin the Catholic University, with the prominent English convert, John Henry Newman, as rector. It was based in the Georgian building on St. Stephen's Green, now known as Newman House. Another legacy is the neighbouring University Church, already mentioned. Eventually, in 1879, in an effort to resolve the controversial issues arising from the Queen's University, this was replaced by the Royal University. The Catholic University became part of the Royal University and it was then reconstituted as the University College, Dublin (UCD). In 1908, on the dissolution of the Royal University, UCD became part of the newly-established National University of Ireland.

Chapter 4
The Wheels of Industry

The coming of the railway and steamship opened up Dublin and Ireland to competition from Britain, the most powerful economy in the world. Dublin's industry, in the main, did not prosper much during the nineteenth century. Unlike the rapidly-growing cities of Britain and indeed, Belfast, Dublin's industry scarcely grew at all. There were some notable exceptions, in brewing and distilling. The city developed also into the banking and commercial capital of Ireland and grandiose monuments to Mammon were built.

As it turned out, the Victorian era was not particularly kind to Dublin in economic terms. The city was part of an economy that was different from, but connected to, the general rural Irish economy. As we have been sharply reminded by recent events, every century can experience severe reversals of economic fortune, and this was certainly true of nineteenth-century Ireland. A period of high demand for agricultural produce during the Napoleonic Wars was followed by a depression. There was, in turn, growth in agriculture, with expansion of areas for tillage, and the relatively new crop, the potato, became dominant. This was allied to a growth in the country's population. Then came the shock of the Famine of the 1840s. An agrarian depression in 1860 was followed by an improvement, and by 1870 an economic boom, spurred by the demand arising from the Franco-Prussian War. An agricultural depression began in 1877. This continued into the 1890s, when economic activity picked up somewhat. Against the background of these ups and downs, Dublin's economy was entwined with that of Britain, which had become the 'workshop of the world.' It proved to be an ill-starred embrace: Dublin's economy did not perform well relative to that of the developing industrial cities of Britain, or with the stellar growth of Belfast's industry. As mentioned previously, Dublin slipped from being the second city of the Empire at the beginning of the nineteenth century to a mere tenth place by the end of it.

By mid-century, the development and then rapid expansion of the railways, as well as the growth of steam-powered cross-channel shipping, radically changed the dynamics of Dublin trade. Most of the railway lines in Ireland radiated from the capital. The railway companies in Ireland and in Britain offered cheap through-freight rates. British goods could now be transported efficiently and cheaply to rural Ireland. In turn, agricultural produce from the country, much of it live cattle, could be easily transported to Dublin for export. Dublin became the *entrepôt*, the trading centre where the orbits of the Irish agricultural hinterland and the powerful adjacent British economy intersected. Local manufacturers found it difficult to compete with mass-produced British products. Dublin, however, did possess an industrial core, which had weaknesses and strengths, and we shall look at some of its main constituents.

Dublin had many traditional industries in 1800. There was substantial manufacture of luxury goods which had catered for the needs of the aristocracy. This included silk, glassmaking and silverware. After the Act of Union, these industries experienced a sharp decline as their main customers abandoned the city and set up in London. Carriage-making represented a substantial part of this sector: it employed 2,000 people in 1800. However, its decline was gradual as carriage-makers diversified from the custom-made carriage to produce a dazzling variety of horse-drawn vehicles, including broughams, landaus, dog carts, jaunting cars, vans and cabs. Dublin-made carriages were in use in Britain, America and India. The coach-building firm of Hutton's built the Irish State Coach (still used in London by the monarch at the opening of Parliament). This was purchased by Queen Victoria and was exhibited at the Great Exhibition held at Leinster Lawn in 1853. Despite such successes, the Dublin coach-building workforce decreased to only around 500 by the last decades of the nineteenth century.

Right. Numerous mills and other industries took advantage of the several rivers which flow through Dublin to the sea. Here, by the Dodder, is a chimney which was part of the former Dublin laundry, now demolished. To the left the nine-arch Milltown Viaduct of the Harcourt Street Railway dating from the mid-nineteenth century, which now carries the Luas light rail system.

Right. Throughout the Victorian era, water power continued to be important for the mills on Dublin's rivers. When the Bohernabreena reservoirs were built in the 1880s near the source of the river Dodder, the 'Millers' Gauge' (seen here, still working) was installed there provide a secure regular flow for the mills on the river.

Near right. A former mill with chimney. It is located by the Camac river near Rowerstown Lane in Kilmainham.

Far right. Shandon Park Mills, Phibsboro, as seen some decades ago, by the Royal Canal. A canal-side location provided convenient transport links.

The Guinness Brewery was the shining success story of industrial Dublin. It provided a high-quality product which catered for the growing demand for porter. Highly mechanised and efficient, it capitalised on improved steamship connections and exported to Britain. By the end of the nineteenth century, it was the largest brewery in the world.

Left. Tracks of the narrow-gauge railway which transported beer kegs to steamers on the Liffey and thence to Dublin Docks for export.

Right. From James Joyce's 'Ulysses', referring to the Guinness Lords Iveagh and Ardilaun: '... they garner the succulent berries of the hop and mass and sift and bruise and brew them and they mix therewith sour juices and bring the must to the sacred fire and cease not night or day from their toil.' A scene from the 1980s: serried ranks of oak vats in Vathouse 4, used for maturation of the Guinness stout before it was racked into casks for distribution.

Left. A view on the top floor of the Robert Street malthouse, built in the mid-1880s, showing the tops of the barley storage bins which make up the core of the building.

The popularity of the dark brew resulted in the Guinness family becoming rich beyond the dreams of Croesus. Members of the Guinness family set up large estates in the Dublin area. In addition, they were generous benefactors. They lavished funds in Victorian Dublin on civic works, workers' housing and the reconstruction of St. Patrick's Cathedral.

Top left. In 1835 Sir Benjamin Lee Guinness established a large estate at St. Anne's in Raheny. It is now a city park. Seen here are the stables at St. Anne's, which date from 1886, and were established by Sir Benjamin's son, Lord Ardilaun.

At the start of the Victorian era, water provided the motive power for Dublin industry. There was a large number of mills and other facilities along the banks of the Dodder, Camac and Liffey. Included were textile manufacture, paper making, iron foundries, saw and flour mills. Water supply, sometimes erratic, was always a concern. At times, mills had to cease production due to water shortages. Towards the end of the nineteenth century, the mill owners on the Dodder objected to the development of the new reservoir at Bohernabreena. To cater for their concerns, a reservoir, separate from the potable water supply, was built and the 'Millers' Gauge' (still in place today) was installed, which guaranteed a minimum flow along the river. With the passage of time, market demand and technology changed and the number of mills declined. The abolition of any remaining duties that protected Irish industries in 1824, in line with the free trade terms of the Act of Union, was particularly harmful to Dublin textile manufacturers.

Ringsend, then remote from the main city and with easy access to shipping, was where some of the grimier industrial processes were located. These included foundries, chemical works and glass making. Many glass manufacturers were located there, producing bottles for the local brewing and distilling industries. As the century continued, there was much industrial development on the other side of the Liffey at North Wall. Coupled with the extension of the port, the slob-lands were filled in and large tracts of ground became available for industrial use. Makers of artificial manure, W. & H. M. Goulding, set up a

Left. Terracotta and red brick at the stables, St. Anne's.

Right. Now regrettably defaced by graffitti, this roof-top Roman tower was moved from the main residence at St. Anne's (demolished in 1943) and placed on a hill above a lake, on the estate, when the house was remodelled in the 1870s. The tower is said to heve been designed by Sir Benjamin Lee Guinness, based on the cenotaph of the Julii (dating from Roman Gaul) at St. Rémy in France.

Below. Clock and cherubs gracing the four-storey Clock Tower at St. Anne's. It contains a giant bell, dated 1850, which carries Sir Benjamin Lee Guinness's initials and the family motto: 'Spes Mea in Deo', or, 'My hope is in God.'

Right. The Farmleigh Estate, near the Phoenix Park, was purchased in 1873 by Sir Benjamin's other son, Edward Cecil Guinness, later Lord Iveagh. This Italianate clock-tower dates from 1880. It houses a water-tank, the water being pumped up from the nearby Strawberry Beds. The clock has two faces, each with a diameter of over four metres. It was made by Grubb, the instrument- and telescope-makers of Rathmines.

Left. Entrance to the Courtyard at Farmleigh.

Above. Entrance hall at Iveagh House, on the south side of St. Stephen's Green. Sir Benjamin Lee Guinness purchased this Georgian house in 1856. It was extensively remodelled in an exuberant style. Now the Department of Foreign Affairs HQ.

Left. Ceramic flowers: the fountain in St. Stephen's Green. Sir Benjamin's son, Lord Ardilaun, funded the reconstruction of St. Stephen's Green during the 1870s.

Right. Airy and grand, the enormous late-Victorian Ballroom of Iveagh House. It is said that the large and glittering social gatherings held here outshone those held by the Lord Lieutenant.

Whiskey distilling was a substantial industry in Victorian Dublin. There were several large distill-eries around the city. Dublin distillers favoured the pot-still method, which gave a finer whiskey

Left. Dominating the square at Smithfield, a boilerhouse chimney, dat-ing from 1895, of the for-mer Jameson Distillery. The photograph was taken in the late 1980s and, other than the chimney it-self, most of the surround-ing buildings have been demolished and replaced by contemporary build-ings, which sadly, are not ageing well.

Below. Offices and Counting House of the former Power's Distillery, on Thomas Street. It dates from 1897 with later ad-ditions.

works there in 1869, which connected with the Liffey wharves by means of a tramway.

Brewing was the success story of industrial Dublin in the nineteenth century. Up to then, spirits had been the preferred beverage of rural Ireland. Beer was more to urban tastes. This was difficult to transport very far on the roads of the time, and consequently there were many local breweries. In 1794, in an effort to reduce drunkenness, taxes were removed from beer in order to encourage consumption away from spirits. In 1799, porter (popular with porters at Covent Garden in London, hence the name), a dark beer with a creamy head, was brewed by the Dublin brewer Arthur Guinness. It soon became the most important product of Irish breweries. At the beginning of the nineteenth century, there were over 50 breweries listed in Dublin. Guinness soon became the largest brewery in the city. Sales within Ireland expanded (facilitated by the

Above. At the former Power's Distillery (now the National College of Art and Design), three of the original stills encased in braced brick, surmounted by copper domes.

Right. As seen in the 1980s, part of the Jones's Road premises, dating from the 1870s, of the Dublin Whiskey Distillery. The building is now much altered and converted into apartments.

expanding railway network). The brewery also developed a large export market.
By the mid-nineteenth century the brewery was producing 100,000 barrels of
beer annually. Thirty years later this had grown to around 750,000 barrels. The
company invested in machinery and continually improved productivity, the
better to cater for its expanding markets. In the 1870s a large expansion and
modernisation programme was initiated. By the next decade the lucky
workforce was over 2,500, enjoying steady and well-paid employment. By the
end of the Victorian era, the massive Guinness complex, which included its own
narrow-gauge railway system, extended to over 50 acres. Offering a mass-
produced high-quality product, it was then the largest brewery in the world.

Over the decades, there was rationalisation of Dublin breweries with some
being absorbed by Guinness. By around 1890, apart from Guinness's, there were
five other breweries. These were: D'Arcy's Anchor Brewery in Usher Street (its
claim was to be 'the largest brewery in Ireland – bar one'); Phoenix and
Manders & Powell, both located in James's Street; Watkins of Ardee Street and
the City of Dublin Brewery in Blackpitts.

Distilling was an old-established industry in Dublin – there were 25
distilleries in 1800. Whiskey was a native product with a well-established and
appreciative market throughout Ireland. At the beginning of Victoria's reign,
whiskey was at its peak – over 12 million gallons were consumed in 1838.
However, in reaction to this Bacchanalian intake of alcohol, Father Mathew
launched his temperance campaign and held his first meeting in Dublin in
1840. This campaign, together with the effects of the Famine and higher spirit
duties, reduced consumption to a third by the 1860s. Innovation came in the
form of the patent-still process, developed by the Irishman Aeneas Coffey in

*Above. Former Mallet
Ironworks at Ninth Lock
on the Royal Canal.
Right. Inchicore Railway
Workshops, founded in
the mid-nineteenth cen-
tury, became the most ad-
vanced centre of
engineering in Ireland at
that time.
Below. Doric columns
supporting the railway
bridge at Sheriff Street,
made by Courtney,
Stephens & Bailey.*

Unlike most British cities, where during the Second World War, many iron railings were removed, Dublin still enjoys a fine array of Victorian ironwork.

Left. Ubiquitous, a little corroded, still elegant, cast-iron railings of a Dublin Victorian house.

Right. There was a pleasant variety in the styles of railings. This example is from Crosthwaite Park in Dún Laoghaire.

Far left. The solid cast iron of this Corinthian capital at Inchicore Railway Works.

Near left. The solid and firm grip of the cast-iron hand at Earlsfort Terrace, in front of what is now the National Concert Hall. The perimeter wall and ironwork date from the Irish International Exhibition, held in 1872.

Right. Examples of Victorian ironwork: elaborate gate at St. Anne's, Raheny; delicate cast iron at Mount Jerome Cemetery.

Left. Details: gatehouse, Ordnance Survey, Phoenix Park; cast-iron downpipe at Portrane Asylum (now St. Ita's).

Right. Mallet's Ironworks provided the railings on the Nassau Street perimeter of Trinity College. Railings from Turner's Ironworks can be seen at the College Street side.

Above. Delicate tracery in wrought iron on an external wall of the Kildare Street Club.

Top left. Wrought iron became popular for gates and fencing towards the end of the Victorian era. This is an artistic example on a gate at the side of the Rathmines Town Hall.

Left. Solid, cast in larger, flatter, sections, late-Victorian cast-iron railings at house on Eglinton Road in Donnybrook.

Right. Poetry in stone and iron, part of the dramatic entrance gates to Howth Castle and Demesne. The ornate cast-iron decoration of the gate is in harmony with the limestone pillar crowned with carved tracery.

Below. Door entrances flanked by repeated spiral patterns in Victorian cast iron.

Left. An impressive symphony of red-brick polychromy at the City Fruit and Vegetable Market at St. Michan's Street. It was designed by Parke Neville in 1891-92.

Left. An opportunity to observe the diet of the Victorian city. Set around the perimeter wall of the City Market is an extravaganza of terracotta detail of foods, which include fish, fruit and vegetables. Here are examples of fish and rhubarb.

The Sunlight Chambers on Essex Quay were built for Lever Brothers and date from 1899-1901. Ceramic decorations depict the manufacture and use of soap in a Renaissance setting. This unites the Victorian virtues of hard work and industry, with presumably, a subtext of cleanliness.
Above left. Men at work: planning and construction. Left. Washerwomen toil as a cherub plays music.

1830. This was more efficient, with significant savings in fuel, but it resulted in a blander whiskey. While the patent-still method was adopted in the north of Ireland, Dublin distillers were conservative and resisted its introduction, preferring the older pot-still method, which produced a finer whiskey. Dublin distilleries were large: John Jameson's Distillery at Bow Street extended over two blocks with a multitude of buildings including grain stores, maltings, kilns, pot-still houses and cooperages. Roe's Distillery in Thomas Street contained the two largest mash tuns in these islands. Other firms were William Jameson's Distillery of Marrowbone Lane and Power's Distillery in John's Lane. The Dublin Whiskey Distillery built a distillery at Jones's Road in the 1870s. Competition from patent-still whiskey forced it to merge in 1889 with the Dublin distillers, William Jameson and George Roe.

The biscuit firm of W. & R. Jacob opened a factory in Peter's Row in 1851. Like Cadbury's and Rowntree's in England, the Jacob family were Quakers. They were in the right market at the right time. The biscuit proved to be a popular food in Victorian times. A contemporary guide noted that the visitor to the factory would be astonished 'to observe the complicated machines required to bring so apparently simple an article of diet to perfection.' In 1885, the cream cracker was developed by Jacobs. The company grew and exported to Britain. It was a very large factory by Dublin standards. Even though the plant was heavily mechanised, over 2,000 people were employed at the end of the nineteenth century.

There were over 100 bakeries in Dublin during the early years of Victoria's reign. Most were small and catered for the needs of their locality. As time passed there was a trend towards consolidation. Johnston, Mooney & O'Brien was formed in 1889 by the amalgamation of three of the largest bakeries. Boland's of Capel Street, another large bakery, adopted new technology and mechanised heavily towards the end of the century. It also had a very large flour mill at the Grand Canal Docks.

Railways were to the forefront of nineteenth-century engineering. The foremost exemplar in Dublin was the Great Southern & Western Railway works in Inchicore. Established in 1846, it was a self-contained world employing the most advanced technology of the time. In this centre of engineering excellence was to be found all the equipment necessary to maintain and construct locomotives and rolling stock, including a sawmill, paint shops, foundry, smithy and boiler shops. Other railway companies were also at the cutting edge of engineering. One of the first locomotives in the world to be built by a railway company in its own workshops was the 'Princess', manufactured at the Grand Canal Street works of the Dublin & Kingstown Railway in 1841. The Midland Great Western Railway also constructed steam locomotives in its works at Broadstone.

Much of the engineering industry in Dublin was at a relatively modest level, manufacturing small items or providing maintenance and repair services. In comparison with Belfast, shipbuilding was on a much smaller scale in Dublin. Traditionally, shipbuilding had been carried out in Ringsend. When a new graving dock was constructed at North Wall in 1859 small ships were built there by Walpole, Webb & Bewley. Towards the end of the century, shipbuilding tailed off there, but enjoyed a brief revival during the twentieth century.

Below. A Victorian tower block: the former Bewley, Moss & Co. Sugar Refinery at Grand Canal Quay, which dates from 1862. With an internal iron frame, it is said to be the first industrial building to utilise this type of iron structure in Ireland.

Dublin had engineering pioneers who produced innovative high-quality products. Richard Turner, ironmaster, of the Hammersmith Works in Ballsbridge, was a leader in the design and manufacture of large glass structures. These were crafted from some of the fruits of the Industrial Revolution, wrought and cast iron and glass, which were now readily available. One of Turner's early works was the Palm House, of 1839, in Belfast. Turner then worked on the great structure, which has been described as one of the finest plant houses in the world. With Decimus Burton, he designed the Great Palm House at Kew Gardens near London, and constructed it in the period 1844 to 1848. Dubliners are fortunate to have the Curvilinear Range building in the National Botanic Gardens in Glasnevin, built mainly by Turner between 1843 and 1869, and expertly renovated by the Office of Public Works in 1995. This building is an example of the decorous use of wrought and cast iron. A large rectangular building, it is attached to lower houses with graceful rounded ends. The whole framework is supported at intervals by cast-iron columns. Decorative pieces, again in cast iron, adorn the roof, eaves and doors. Turner used his expertise in large-span roofs for railway stations, constructing the original roof of Broadstone Station in 1847, as well as a roof for Liverpool's Lime Street railway station. The boom in railway construction proved a blessing for engineering firms in Dublin. The Dublin engineering works of John & Robert Mallet made the roofs of several Dublin termini, including that of the Dublin & Drogheda Railway at Amiens Street (now Connolly Station), as well as the passenger shed at Kingsbridge (now Heuston Station) for the Great Southern & Western Railway. The firm supplied many products for the railways from bolts and fastenings, to cranes and turntables. They also designed and constructed roofs for railway stations in England in the mid-1850s. Robert Mallet (1810-81) was a polymath: an engineer and scientist. Amongst his many innovations were a huge mortar designed for the Crimean War and the structural use of buckled plates for bridge decks. He collaborated in developing the seismograph (a word which he coined, along with 'seismology') to study earthquake effects and used this to measure the shockwaves from exploding charges placed on Killiney beach in 1849.

Courtney, Stephens & Bailey of Blackhall Place was another firm that benefitted from the railway boom. Originally coachbuilders, it had built carriage bodies for the Dublin & Kingstown Railway. It supplied many railway bridges including the wrought-iron bridge over the River Nore at Thomastown in 1877, which replaced the timber lattice girder bridge built there by Mallets. The firm provided the ironwork in 1872 for Grattan Bridge in Dublin. Various sections of the railings that enclose Trinity College offer a felicitous opportunity to observe the work of the three great nineteenth-century Dublin engineering works of Turner, Mallet and Courtney, Stephens & Bailey.

Innovation was at the heart of the Grubb telescope works south of the Grand Canal in Rathmines, a district not generally known as an industrial heartland. The 'Optical and Mechanical Works' were located off Lower Rathmines Road. As well as making clocks, the firm had developed a mastery in the intricate instrumentation of telescopes and the manufacture and grinding of lenses. Large, sophisticated telescopes were exported, including those for observatories in Europe, Australia and South Africa. In 1875, the firm secured a contract to

Right. The South telescope at Dunsink Observatory, which is located to the north of Dublin. Erected there in 1868, the telescope is still in working order. It uses a 12-inch lens cast in Paris in 1829 (it was then the largest lens in the world) which was later donated by the renowned English astronomer Sir James South. It was set in an 1853 telescope mounting by Thomas Grubb. The Grubb Optical and Mechanical Works in Rathmines also provided the dome enclosure with a rotating opening mechanism. The Grubb Works was a thriving hub of advanced optical technology during the nineteenth century. It produced astronomical telescopes (including the casting and polishing of glass lenses) which were exported all over the world. In 1875, the Imperial Royal Observatory of Austro-Hungary placed an order with the firm for a 27-inch telescope, which was then the largest refracting telescope in the world. Instruments like clocks and seismographs were also manufactured. Later, the firm produced periscopes for the British Admiralty, supplying 95% of Royal Navy submarines during the First World War.

Right. Two views of the mechanical mechanism at the base of the Dunsink telescope. This equatorial driving clock allows an adjustable and accurate drive rate.

GRUBB
1868
DUBLIN

Heat and lighting were provided to the Victorian city by gas. Gas was distributed throughout the city by a maze of underground pipes.

Two views from the 1980s, at the the Alliance and Dublin Consumers' Gas Company premises: Above, the gas holder of 1885, along South Lotts Road. Note the detail at the top of the column – Victorian engineering usually included decorative touches. Top right, since demolished, the gas distributor house, in a state of dereliction.

Left. Apartments now fill the frame of the 1885 gas holder.

Right. The city's first electricity-generating station was set up in 1881. Seen here, Dublin Corporation's generating station at the Pigeon House in Ringsend, begun in 1901.

supply a 27-inch telescope for Vienna. This was the largest refracting telescope in the world. At the end of the nineteenth century, the firm began making periscopes for submarines for the British Admiralty. Grubb went on to supply around 95% of the periscopes for British submarines during the First World War. After the 1916 rising, the British Admiralty, worried about security of supply, insisted that production be carried out in Britain. There is no vestige of the Grubb works now left in Rathmines except the street name 'Observatory Lane.' However, a Grubb telescope is still operational at Dunsink Observatory.

In Dublin, as gas street-lights replaced oil lamps during the 1820s, three gas companies emerged. One of the these, the Dublin Oil Gas Company, of Great Brunswick (now Pearse) Street, produced gas from whale oil. After the gas works there ceased production, the building became the Antient Concert Rooms in 1847, later becoming the Academy Cinema. The three gas companies were in competition with each other, sometimes laying mains side by side along the same street. Tales, perhaps apocryphal, recount that there was a common practice in gas companies to pay clandestine bonuses to foremen. These quietly connected customers to a rival gas line, while the company continued to bill the customers. Consolidation occurred among the companies and an English-owned monopoly gas provider emerged. In 1844, a meeting was held by concerned citizens, chaired by the then Lord Mayor Daniel O'Connell, who

Below. In Harry Street, the former Weights and Measures Office, constructed for Dublin Corporation in 1880.

Right. The area around Dame Street and College Green became the commercial and financial heart of Victorian Dublin. Here, the buildings were of import and substance, usually with fine detailing and often a touch of fantasy.

Right. The sandstone and copper-green turret of the former Commercial Union Assurance Co. building at the corner of Grafton Street and College Green. Completed in 1885 to a design by Thomas Newenham Deane and his son Thomas Manly Deane.

Near right. detail from the former Scottish Widows Insurance building (1875) at the corner of College Street (now an AIB bank). Constructed in Scottish ochre sandstone, to a design by Thomas Newenham Deane.

Far right. Carved detail surrounds a window of the former Provincial Bank (1868) on College Street, now the Westin Hotel.

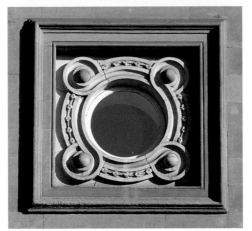

Left. Victorian banking at its grandest: the Banking Hall of the former Royal Bank (latterly AIB, now owned by Trinity College) at Foster Place. It dates from 1860. Decorated cast-iron columns support the barrel-vaulted ceiling of this high and airy space.

Below, far left. Cast-iron pillars form an advance guard in front of the former National Bank at College Green, which was founded by Daniel O'Connell. The original building dates from 1845.

Below, near left. Patriotism made manifest atop the National Bank. Here are national symbols of the nineteenth century: Hibernia with a harp is flanked by a wolfhound; shamrocks and crowns abound.

Right. The former Munster Bank (now AIB) on Dame Street. Thomas Newenham Deane brought echoes of Lombardy in this design to the prosaic world of nineteenth-century Irish banking. It dates from 1873.

Near right. The arms of Cork and Dublin appear on this medallion of Portland stone set in the limestone exterior of the former Munster Bank.

Far right. Part of the rich stucco decoration in the Munster Bank.

Left. The Banking Hall of the former Union Bank (now NIB) on Dame Street, which dates from 1867. It was the headquarters of the former Hibernian Bank. The stucco ceiling is wonderful and one of the best in Victorian Dublin.

Below left. Well-proportioned barrel vault ceiling at the entrance to the Ulster Bank on College Green. It dates from 1891, designed by Sir Thomas Drew.

Below. Elaborate carving at the entrance to the NIB Bank. Charles Harrison carved the exquisite array of stone decoration to be found on the bank.

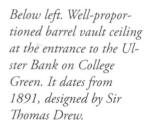

Right, Thomas Newenham Deane once again brought north Italy to Dame Street with his design for Crown Life Insurance, dating from 1868. The stepped arcade on Fownes Street faces the Central Bank plaza. Insurance in nineteenth-century Dublin was dominated by British insurance companies, which established local offices in the city.

Near right. Prominent at the apex of Westmoreland and D'Olier Streets, the former Liverpool & Lancashire Insurance building, dating from 1898. It was designed by J. J. O'Callaghan.

Far right. Carved crest on the Liverpool & Lancashire Insurance building.

Commercial symphonies in red brick. Brick was popular for shops, public houses, arcades and offices during the late-Victorian era. Bricks were cheap, easy to make and, as we see, buildings could be erected in versatile shapes.

Left. In Scottish Baronial style: with a turret projecting over the corner entrance, this building in Rathmines was built for the Belfast Banking Company in 1901.

Right. Ruritania brought to South Great George's Street. The fantastical turrets of the South City Markets, in red brick and terracotta. The building dates from 1878, and was restored in 1892 after a fire. Along with Monster (or Department) Stores, arcades proved a popular way to display and sell the consumer products of the Industrial Revolution.

Near right. At the South City Markets (now George's Street Arcade): cast-iron brackets with a heraldic theme.
Far right. All Gothic Revival, the turrets flank the entrance.

Left. With an ornate copper dome over yellow terracotta and red brick, this store for Todd Burns (now Penneys), in Mary Street, dates from 1902-5

Above. Detail from timber fascia of this 1890s commercial building in Anglesea Street.

Above left. The Flemish Gothic stair-turret of this building (now Bruxelles Pub) in Harry Street, which dates from around 1890 to a design by J. J. O'Callaghan.

Left. A relic of Switzer's Department Store (now Brown Thomas) on Wicklow Street, with lettering in gold mosaic.

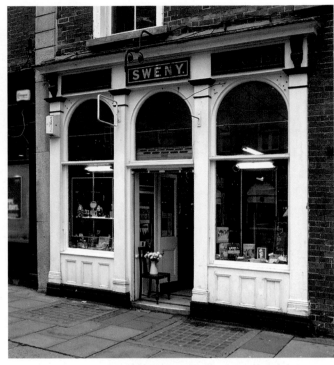

Above. In Monkstown on Carrickbrennan Road, a traditional timber-fronted shopfront, set against red brick with polychrome detailing.

Above right. The modest traditional shopfront of Sweny's Pharmacy of Lincoln Place, where, in 'Ulysses', Leopold Bloom purchased his soap of 'sweet lemony wax.'

Near right. Anglesea Street was the the hub of Victorian stockbroking in Dublin. Here is an elaborate stucco and timber-fronted mélange dating from 1898.

Far right. On Dawson Street, the gables of Drummond's store (now Hodges Figgis) in Dutch Revival red brick and terracotta (1903).

Left. Cleary's Public House in Inchicore presents the classical Victorian timber frontage with the name displayed prominently in gold paint on the fascia over the windows. Thirsty men from the nearby Great Southern & Western Railway Works, were, no doubt, inspired by their company's name which is displayed on high.

Right. The traditional wooden partitions, mirrors and alluring snug of Doheny and Nesbitt's on Baggot Street, said to be founded in 1850.

Left. Kavanagh's (known as the Gravedigger's) is a Victorian public house conveniently adjacent to the Prospect Square entrance to Glasnevin Cemetery. The first proprietor, John Kavanagh, is said to have had 25 children, three of whom went to fight in the American Civil War during the 1860s.

Below. The Palace Bar on Fleet Street which dates from around 1890.

resolved to set up an alternative. By 1847 a new company duly emerged, the Alliance and Dublin Consumers' Gas Company. Gas was produced at that time by placing coal in retorts and heating it to around 1,000 degrees Fahrenheit. There was a large works adjacent to Barrow Street and South Lotts Road from which gas was carried to all parts of the city by a complex network of piping. By mid-century gas began to be used for domestic cooking and heating. In 1884, Dublin had 3,750 street gas lamps, attended by 23 gas lighters.

The Nelson Pillar was lit to demonstrate the new-fangled concept of electricity (most likely using arc lights) on the occasion of Queen Victoria's visit in 1849. It was due to developments such as the invention of the incandescent light bulb that, in 1880, a single electric light was used for street lighting outside the offices of the *Freeman's Journal* in Prince's Street in Dublin. In 1881, the Dublin Electric Light Company established a generating station at Schoolhouse Lane. Initially it supplied lamps on the streets around Kildare Street and up to St. Stephen's Green. Anticipating a competitive threat, the Gas Company established its generating station at Hawkins Street in 1890 which supplied the shopping areas of Grafton, Georges and Henry Streets. Convinced of the advantages of electric light, Dublin Corporation set up its own generating station at Fleet Street in 1892. This provided electricity, not just for street lighting, but also for individual consumers. Demand increased and the Corporation decided to set up a large generating station in the Pigeon House Fort, which it had acquired from the War Office. Work began in 1901. When completed in 1903, it had a power output of 3,000 kilowatts and supplied the

153

city via 20 new substations. As the twentieth century dawned, Dublin had
entered the age of electricity.

Dublin was the financial and commercial centre of Ireland. The Irish Stock
Exchange was established there after a 1799 bill that regulated stockbrokers.
Early transactions included Irish Government debt and canal shares. By 1844
there were 44 joint-stock companies listed in Ireland, a figure that was to rise to
nearly 3,000 by the 1880s. The Bank of Ireland was established in 1783, and
initially did not operate outside Dublin. Restrictive legislation resulted in
banking outside Dublin being confined to small private banks. Liberalisation of
the banking law in the 1820s resulted in the establishment of a wave of large
joint-stock banks. The Northern Bank was founded in Belfast in 1824. In 1825,
the Hibernian and Provincial Banks were set up. Daniel O'Connell's National
Bank was founded in 1835, the Royal and Ulster Banks in 1836. The Munster
Bank (transformed in 1885 into the Munster and Leinster) was set up in 1862.
Dublin was the outpost for English and Scottish insurance companies, which
dominated the Irish market. Irish headquarters for these companies were
established in the city, the main business being life and fire insurance.

The area centred on Dame and College Streets is the beneficiary of nineteenth-century expansion in financial services. Walk up Dame Street today and
observe how the worthies of Victorian finance were able to convert silver into
stone. Standing with the Georgian neo-classicism of the Bank of Ireland at one's
back, one can savour the architectural blend of fantasy and medievalism of the
banks and insurance companies all along Dame Street. Financial institutions
had the wherewithal to build solid and expensive buildings. Banks were built
displaying much decoration, be it terracotta, stone carving or stucco. In the
slightly ethereal world of finance, confidence (fairly dented in Ireland's banks
today) is all. The Victorian banks of Dame Street were built to inspire that
confidence. These buildings are impressive and substantial: observe a turret here,
Italianate stone carving there, and ornate decoration all over. In rapid succession
we have: the former National Bank (currently unoccupied), topped by the
appropriate patriotic symbols of shamrocks, Hibernia with harp, round tower

Below. Eyecatching: the
late-Victorian frontage of
Cassidy's on Camden
Street.

Right. Proudly proclaiming its presence: with its lamp-holding bronze arms, Neary's Public House on Chatham Street, dating from around 1900.

Right. The Long Hall, in South Great George's Street, retains its traditional Victorian interior. It is said that the pub was closed temporarily in 1867, when the hunt was on for those involved in the Fenian uprising.

and wolfhound; the Italianate classical Ulster Bank (Thomas Drew, 1883), with its fine entrance porch still intact and the National Irish Bank (completed 1867, formerly the Hibernian Bank, then purchased by the Northern Bank) with carved stonework by C. W. Harrison and a magnificent banking hall with elaborate coved ceiling. Over at 3 Foster Place, in the former Royal Bank, the banking hall is well lit and lofty; the barrelled roof is supported by decorated cast-iron columns. Venetian Gothic was the style employed by Thomas Newenham Deane for the Munster (now AIB) Bank dating from 1873, at the junction of Dame Street and Palace Street. In grey limestone, its style is similar to that employed in Deane and Woodward's Museum Building in Trinity College. Deane, son of Sir Thomas Deane, had also worked on that project. The former Crown Life Insurance building (now a hotel) on Dame Street and at the corner of Fownes Street, beside the Central Bank, is also by Deane. It dates from 1868 and its Venetian palazzo style is exuberantly remote from the staid world of actuarial tables.

Fantasy also abounded in the trading and commercial world. Close by in South Great George's Street (at the South City Markets) there is a vigorous example of a Victorian arcade which dates from 1878 and rebuilt after a fire in 1892. Built of red brick and terracotta, it has a marvellously turreted style reminiscent of the castles of the mad King Ludwig of Bavaria. Over the nineteenth century most of the city-centre commercial area was remodelled. Many of the buildings of the previous century were rebuilt or refaced. In Georgian times shops were small and usually sold one commodity. As time progressed shops became larger. The easier availability of cheaper plate glass enabled a shop to present an expansive glass frontage. Arcaded markets had been popular from the early 1800s. The department store (also known as 'Monster' stores), a French innovation, came into prominence from the mid-nineteenth century onwards. These offered a greater quantity and variety of goods, mostly from British factories, and not of local manufacture. Brown Thomas, founded in 1848, was the principal store of the fashionable shopping area, Grafton Street. It was noted in the 1880s that it had buyers in the Parisian and German markets who obtained the latest fashions. It copied and sold these, to great appreciation from its fashion-conscious customers. Copyright law must have been lax. A contemporary publication noted 'this step ... practically takes the wind out of the sails of the foreigner.' The adjacent Switzers, founded in 1838, was another large department store (to which Brown Thomas has moved in recent decades). Arnott & Company's Drapery store was a large establishment in Henry Street. Sir John Arnott, the Managing Director, was owner of the *Irish Times* and was also engaged in housing development. The present frontage dates from 1894. Pim Brothers & Company's establishment in Great George's Street sold poplin, the produce of their own factory. The store was tall and well lit, with arcades to each side and with extensive counters ranging along the length of the main floor. In 1883, a Mr J. Clery purchased a large department store, the Dublin Drapery Warehouse, in Sackville (now O'Connell) Street, which continues to bear his name.

Victorian Dublin saw much growth in the numbers of its public houses and grocery shops. Many of these were set up by Catholic migrants from the country, usually financed using the capital of their farms. In time, vintners and

Above. Stained-glass window in the Stag's Head Public House in Dame Court, which dates from 1890.

Below. Grand and imposing at the north-east of St. Stephen's Green, the large Victorian pile of the Shelbourne Hotel. This dates from 1865. John McCurdy was the architect, fresh from his designing of the extension to Kilmainham Gaol, with its markedly more Spartan quarters.

*Right. A Nubian slave
girl lights the front of the
Shelbourne Hotel. One of
a series of four figures of
princesses and slaves, these
were cast in a Paris stu-
dio. Local wits, at the
time, claimed that these
were the only four virgins
left in Dublin.*

grocers became dominant groups in Dublin Corporation. The temperance movement found the spread of public houses to be distasteful. Frederick Stokes, the driving force behind Rathmines Township, also found the rise of taverns to be objectionable and disagreed with the granting of publicans' licences there. Today, Victorian examples of that essential Dublin amenity, the public house, can still be seen around the city. In between the expensive (and usually unfortunate) renovations, there are some outstanding traditional public houses still in existence. The exterior is usually ornate, with the owner's name displayed in large letters. The interior is even more ornate, with carved dark woodwork, long mirrors and an atmosphere conducive to allowing the clientele enjoy the wares of the establishment.

Above. A gilt dolphin glares at passers-bys at the entrance to the former Dolphin Hotel on Essex Street. J. J. O'Callaghan designed this 1890s building.

So, while there was economic development in the city, it was nothing on the scale of British cities. Why did Dublin not perform better? Some disadvantages were minor. Despite Ireland's then perceived paucity of mineral resources, iron and coal were cheaply and readily available due to the excellent shipping links with Britain with its efficient railway system. In any case, coal made up only a small part of the cost of operating a factory which made lighter products. One disadvantage was a scarcity of skilled workers, not helped by a lack of local training facilities. Over the years, higher wages were needed to attract these workers from Britain. A certain amount of capital may have been leached out of the country by rents to absentee landlords but there was not an overall lack of finance – by 1860, £60 million had been invested in non-productive but secure shelter in government stock or on deposit with the Irish banks (which in turn deposited much of this in secure deposits in London). However, there was a lack of confidence in Ireland and its prospects. A constant theme in Irish books and periodicals of the Victorian era was a lament about the lack of industry and the need to develop it. One definite disadvantage was that the natural market for potential Dublin-manufactured goods across Ireland, was, after the Famine, suffering a severe decline in population. Dublin, however, had the advantage of being adjacent to the greatest economy the western world had ever known, with ready markets if the right products could be identified. While it was unlikely that there would be opportunities to compete against the huge industrial factories of northern Britain, there were opportunities in Dublin for specialised manufacture of niche products. However, with the exception of a few sectors like brewing, there was a signal lack of entrepreneurial risk-taking and innovation in Ireland. In Victorian society as a whole, trade and commerce were at a lower step on the social ladder. Manufacturing was held in lesser regard, being seen as offering higher risks and greater competition. Many Irish business owners used the profits of their enterprise to buy land, and thus become members of the landed classes. Dublin's religious and historical inheritance may also have militated against the enterprise economy. Much of Dublin's middle class (mainly Protestant) were ensconced in comfortable professional, commercial and civil service employment. The emergent Catholic middle class was striving towards entering the professions of medicine and law. Catholic capital was also directed towards the setting up of public houses and shops. After Catholic Emancipation, a significant part of Catholic economic resources was directed into an exuberant church-building programme. Thus, while many magnificent churches (and banks) of the Victorian era can still be seen in Dublin, there are very few factory buildings dating from that period.

Chapter 5
The Well-Connected City

Dublin was a small, intimate city at the dawn of the nineteenth century. One could walk to most parts of the city. As the suburbs expanded, modes of transport became more sophisticated. The horse-tram network developed and Dublin became a transport hub, connected by railway to most towns and cities by 1865. Good connections and the rise of the steamship contributed to the expansion of Dublin Port. In the Dublin of 1900, it was probably easier to move around the city and suburbs by electric tram or railway, than it is today.

Up to the end of the eighteenth century, transport was primitive. The carts and coaches in use were slow and costly. For Dublin a radical change was the canals that were being built around that time. These improved connections to the rest of the country. Work commenced on the Grand Canal scheme in 1757. The last section, the Circular line from James's Street harbour to Ringsend, was completed in 1796. The more northerly Royal Canal route to the Liffey was opened in 1801. Carrying passengers and freight, the canals linked Dublin to the midlands and to the rivers Shannon and Barrow. However, travelling by canal was slow. It took over 13 hours to travel from Dublin to Athy.

Competition in transport has always been a healthy force. In May 1834, in an effort to compete with coach services, fast 'fly boat' services were established on the Grand Canal. Two horses towed these boats at speeds that averaged six to eight miles per hour. This service lasted only until 1852, as passenger services on the canals were not able to compete with the railways that were being built.

Horsepower had been the principal means for connecting Dublin to the rest of the country. Mail-coach services had been established by 1789. Charles Bianconi, based in Clonmel, began a passenger-coach service in 1815. In the decades that followed, Bianconi and other operators provided regular coach connections across the country, many operating out of Dublin.

Georgian Dublin was bounded by the canals. It was an intimate city and it was possible to walk between the main points of the capital. Horse transport grew in line with the city's expansion and private carriages and public hackneys carried people to and fro. As the nineteenth century proceeded, the city grew larger and developed significantly in a southerly direction. The poor and the lower middle class could not easily afford a cab or carriage. They had to live within walking distance of their employment. Distances increased as the city expanded, and by the mid-century, horse omnibus services were set up. These involved large horse-drawn coaches operating on a predetermined route, running at fixed times. These double-deck vehicles were pulled by two or more horses. Clondalkin, Rathmines, Terenure, Clontarf, Rathfarnham and Sandymount were among the areas served. Fares were low, and patronage grew accordingly. The omnibus service and the subsequent trams liberated the lower middle class, who could now choose to live at a much further distance from their employment.

Rattling along on the iron wheels of an omnibus was not a comfortable way to travel, certainly not on cobblestones or unpaved roads such as those of the new (and parsimonious) Rathmines Township. Indeed, it was the poor state of the streets of the developing cities of the United States that led to the development of horse trams there from 1832 (in New York, by an Irishman, John Stephenson). Despite the appeal of the smooth ride of steel wheel on rail, there was a lag in the development of trams in Europe. The new technology was introduced to Dublin by an American entrepreneur, George F. Train, who, in 1867, laid a demonstration section of rails along Aston Quay. The Corporation decided these were a nuisance and ordered their removal. It was to take until February 1872 before the first Dublin horse tram ran. This operated between College Green and Garville Avenue in Rathgar. These trams, pulled by two horses, were double-deck with the driver and the passengers on the top deck and

Right. Grattan Bridge over the Liffey. Dublin's development was intimately related to the river and its crossings over the centuries. The present Grattan Bridge was rebuilt and widened in 1873-5. Courtney, Stephens & Bailey provided the iron castings for the bridge. Note the similarity of the sea-horse design to that at the entrance to the superintendant's house at Vartry (part of the Vartry Water Scheme by Dublin Corporation) as shown on page 58.

open to the elements. Trams were initially laid mainly to the southern suburbs of the city and catered for a mainly middle-class clientele. As the tramways were private undertakings, this made eminent sense for extracting substantial fares from the passengers. In a letter to the *Freeman's Journal* in March 1878, Maurice Brooks MP criticised the Dublin Tramway Company's elitist approach, while noting that it was 'making excellent returns to the proprietors and proving of great convenience to passengers of the genteel and well-to-do classes.'

In time, the tram network did move from the lucrative southern routes towards the north side and the trams ran along North Circular Road, Parkgate Street and through Drumcondra and Clontarf. The tramway proved to be a spur to development in such areas as Clontarf, which had lagged behind the townships to the south. The line that opened there in 1873 fostered expansion in that area. New houses were built within walking distance of the tramway service. Dublin trams proved popular. 137 tramcars ran on 32 route miles of track by 1881 when three companies amalgamated to form the Dublin United Tramways Company (DUTC). On the eve of electrification a typical fare on the horse tram was threepence from Nelson's Pillar to Clonskeagh. This service ran from 8.00 a.m. to just after 10.00 p.m.

Two steam tramways were constructed in the 1880s (in common with several light steam tramways that were being built on the western seaboard at the time). One ran from Parkgate Street to Lucan; the other from Terenure to Blessington (and later to Poulaphuca) and afforded a means for farmers to bring their produce to the city. These lines generally ran at the side of the road and enjoyed substantial passenger traffic during the summer holiday periods. In 1900, the Lucan line was converted and electrified.

The world's first electric tramway had been developed by Werner von Siemens in Berlin in 1881. This technology spread to the United States and, by July 1890, one sixth of the tramways there were electrified. It was more economical than the heavy cost of maintaining fleets of horses (the DUTC operated a ratio of around ten horses per tram car), not to mind the problem of dispersal of horse manure. Electric trams were faster: with the same number of cars, a greater frequency and greater overall carrying capacity could be obtained. DUTC officials visited locations in Europe to inspect electric tramways. Another delegation, which included the DUTC Chairman William Martin Murphy, visited the United States during the early 1890s. There was opposition to electrification. The Dublin Carmen's Union, representing the jarveys, objected as they feared that the electric trams, unlike the horse trams, would be significantly faster than their vehicles. The Lord Mayor protested, pointing out the loss in growing oats and horse breeding to farmers. The first electric tram was operated from Haddington Road to Dalkey in May 1896 by the Dublin Southern District Tramways Company (DSDT). The 500-volt DC supply was provided by a generating station at Shelbourne Road. The service proved popular and the coastal railway line lost passengers. In a bid to regain patronage the Dublin, Wicklow & Wexford Railway Company opened new stations at Merrion and Sandymount and reduced fares. The DSDT amalgamated with the DUTC in September 1896. Over the next few years, electrification of Dublin's tramways gathered pace and the end of the horse cars was announced in January

Right. The former tramway depot at Dalkey, as seen in the 1980s A horse-tram network was developed across Dublin from the late 1870s. This greatly fostered the expansion of the suburbs. The first electric tram in the Dublin area operated to Dalkey in 1896.

Below. The insignia of the Dublin United Tramway Company, as displayed in the National Transport Museum, Howth.

Left. Near Salthill, the parabolic granite walls of the railway line, shaped to resist the waves from the Irish Sea. The coast from Dublin to Kingstown (now Dún Laoghaire) was defined by the Dublin & Kingstown Railway, built by William Dargan, which opened in December 1834. This was the first suburban railway in the world and marked the start of the railway age in Ireland. By 1865, railways radiated from Dublin to most towns and cities in Ireland.

William Dargan (1799-1867) was known as the 'Father of Ireland's Railways.' He built the first railway to Kingstown and many subsequent Irish railways.

Below left. Tableau of Dargan in his special railway carriage, on display at the Transport Museum at Cultra, near Belfast.

Below. In the former boardroom of the Great Southern & Western Railway at Heuston Station, detail from portrait of Dargan.

Right. Statue of William Dargan in front of the National Gallery on Merrion Square. He had sponsored the 1853 Exhibition of Art and Industry, which was held on Leinster Lawn. Dargan subsequently became the leading protagonist in the establishment of the National Gallery of Ireland. Queen Victoria visited the 1853 Exhibition. During her time in Dublin, she called on Dargan at his residence in Mount Anville. In her eyes, he represented the ideal Irishman and she offered him a knighthood, which he declined.

Below. The world's first commercial use of an atmospheric railway was the Kingstown to Dalkey system that opened in 1844. A vacuum was generated which pulled a piston attached to a small carriage. It was closed in 1854. The powerhouse that generated the vacuum was located at Atmospheric Road in Dalkey.

óthar Atmaisféarach
MOSPHERIC ROAD

1901 when the Sandymount tram line (via the difficult low bridge at Bath Avenue) was finally electrified.

The first railway in Dublin opened just before the dawn of the Victorian age. The Dublin to Kingstown (now Dún Laoghaire) railway was the first suburban railway in the world. Originally a canal had been planned to provide a connection from Dublin to the newly-constructed Kingstown harbour. The silting up of Dublin port meant that larger vessels could not use it, and called at Kingstown instead. As Kingstown grew in importance, the question of a connection with Dublin was discussed. The age of great enthusiasm for railways had begun and, in 1825, a petition was made to the House of Commons proposing a railway. The Dublin and Kingstown Railway Act received Royal assent in September 1831. The first committee meeting was held in November 1831. The professional men and merchant princes of Dublin were represented by names such as Barton, Pim, Ferrier and Roe. Wexford-born Charles Blacker Vignoles, experienced in construction of railways in England, had been appointed as Chief Engineer. William Dargan's tender for constructing the line was accepted. Dargan was to become known as the 'Father of Ireland's Railways', building these across the country in the great expansion that followed. Dargan's legacy of the line to Kingstown – the solid stone bridges, the railway formation and the parabolic sea wall along by the coast – can still be seen today, from the rear of Pearse Station to the termination of the initial line near the West Pier at Dún Laoghaire. The line, to a 4 ft 8½ in gauge (the distance between the running edges of the rails), opened in December 1834. It was planned to continue the line to the south. A new wharf to cater for steamers, including the mail boat, was built to the south of the harbour. The extension to the site of the present Dún Laoghaire station was complete by May 1837, again constructed by Dargan.

The Dublin & Kingstown Railway (D&KR) now began to make arrangements for an extension to the growing township of Dalkey. An innovative scheme was prepared to lay an atmospheric railway there from Kingstown. It followed the route of the quarry tramway recently used during construction of the new harbour. Objections were made to the proposed route but a cutting was eventually built with a series of 'flower bed' bridges to camouflage this. With no locomotive smoke-stack to be coped with, the initial clearance of bridges over the cutting was low. These can be still seen today on the Dún Laoghaire seafront near the Royal Marine Hotel. A cast-iron pipe with a leather flap valve was laid between the rails along the course of the line. A steam engine located in a power house at Dalkey created a vacuum in the pipe. A small carriage was attached to a piston in the pipe. At Kingstown, the brakes would be released and the vacuum would pull the carriage, complete with passengers, up the incline to Dalkey. The return journey was made by gravity. This, the first commercial use of an atmospheric railway to carry passengers, opened in 1844. Advanced technology can be a difficult task. Many problems were experienced with the ox-hide flaps on the atmospheric pipe. Cast-iron plates were laid on the flaps and tallow employed to achieve a seal. However, the vacuum was difficult to maintain. There were frequent failures with the valve. Passenger traffic also dropped off, particularly during the Famine years. The atmospheric line lasted until April 1854. A deeper cutting was excavated for steam traction and a track using the new Irish gauge of 5 ft 3 in installed.

Meanwhile, the great national railway expansion was underway. Throughout the nineteenth century, Belfast raced ahead of Dublin in terms of industrial growth and expansion. And so, in the late 1830s, the next railway was not from Dublin, but from Belfast. Construction of a line out of Belfast began in 1837 and the section to Portadown opened in 1842, operating to a 6 ft 2 in gauge. The concept of a Dublin to Belfast railway had been in vogue since 1825. The Dublin & Drogheda Railway (D&DR) was planned to be part of this route. Disagreements over whether it was to be inland or coastal delayed the building of this line. Work started in 1838 on a short portion from the Royal Canal in Dublin to Portmarnock, directed by the company's engineer, John Macneill. Based on Macneill's advice, the company came to favour a 5 ft 2 in gauge. With the prospect of different gauges, alarm bells began to ring. The Inspector General of Railways, Major-General Pasley, was asked to investigate. He consulted widely and investigated the variety of gauges that had emerged in Britain, which included 5 ft and 5 ft 6 in. After due consultation, he recommended a mean of 5 ft 3 in, which is still the standard gauge throughout

Below. Heavy material, delicate execution: the tracery of these Victorian cast-iron brackets, which support a platform roof at Amiens Street (now Connolly) Station.

Below. Company crest of the Great Northern Railway Board.

Right. In 1844 the Lord Lieutenant laid the foundation stone for the terminus of the Dublin & Drogheda Railway at Amiens Street. The engineer of the line, John Macneill, was then knighted. This Italianate design in grey granite, by William Deane Butler, the least successful of the Dublin termini, is dull and ill-proportioned.

Below right. Red and yellow brick polychromy was the theme for this part of the former headquarters of the Great Northern Railway (Ireland) adjacent to the terminus at Amiens Street. John Lanyon designed the original building which opened in 1879 and was extended in 1884. The building is now the head office of Iarnród Éireann (Irish Rail).

Below. Railway fittings of the Victorian era were highly decorated. Cast-iron medallions on a footbridge (since replaced) at Malahide Station.

167

Right. The original cast-iron columns and spandrels which support the roof over the platforms at Kingsbridge (now Heuston) Station. The platform roof was designed in 1845 by Sir John Macneill. The contractor was William Dargan and the ironwork was provided by J. & R. Mallet.

Left. The corner tower with red brick and sandstone of the former Great Northern Railway (Ireland) headquarters at Amiens Street. The cast-iron pillar is to a rather heavy design, an idiom carried on in the surrounding railings and in the stairs inside the building.

Below. Company crest of the Great Southern & Western Railway (GS&WR).

Top right. The stately façade of Kingsbridge (now Heuston) Station, the terminus of the GS&WR. It dates from 1848, to a design by Sancton Wood. Cupolas on either side give a flavour of the Raj.

Right. The insignia of cities served by the GS & WR adorn the façade of Heuston Station. Here are those of Dublin and Limerick.

Right. Sancton Wood included a tower in his design for the (now former) running shed at the Inchicore Railway Works. It originally provided a point for the signal or 'lookout' men. This arrangement was soon replaced by the castellated signal box seen to the right. Parnell, at a meeting in Inchicore in 1891, praised the men of the works as 'comprising amongst them the best mechanical and engineering talents in Ireland.'

Above. Crane, made by Joseph Adamson & Co. of Hyde, dating from 1901, at Inchicore Works.

Left. Wagons and wheels: at Inchicore, turntable and building near the old running shed.

Ireland. This gauge is also still in use in parts of the Australian and Brazilian railway networks.

Construction continued on the D&DR using the revised gauge and, in March 1844, a train carried the Lord Lieutenant and over 500 passengers from the Royal Canal to Drogheda. Two months later, the same Lord laid the foundation stone for the new terminus at Amiens Street. He followed this ceremony by knighting Macneill. It was to take until 1855 before there was a permanent rail connection from Dublin to Belfast. The reason for the delay was the difficult crossing of the river Boyne. Based on an original concept by Macneill, a great bridge was built across the Boyne valley at Drogheda. The river spans used wrought-iron lattice girders. This was the new material of the time and the railways used the products of the Industrial Revolution with enthusiasm.

Below. The imposing facade of Broadstone Station.

The D&DR opened a branch line to Howth in 1847, with the hope of generating cross-channel traffic out of the harbour. This never materialised. However, there was commuter traffic and this helped the growth of residential Howth. The D&DR actively promoted development in Howth and other areas near its northern line, such as Balbriggan and Malahide. In 1861, there was on offer a free first-class ticket, valid for fifteen years, for each house over a £50 valuation. In those class-conscious times, a house under that valuation would only merit a second-class ticket.

William Deane Butler designed the terminus at Amiens Street (now known as Connolly Station). This grey granite building, albeit a little stolid, has an imposing central Italianate tower. By 1876, the Great Northern Railway (Ireland) was formed, and incorporated most railways to the north of the country. The GNR(I) built its red-brick headquarters at Amiens Street, to a design by John Lanyon and was completed in 1879. It matches the nearby

Right. Writing about Broadstone Station, Maurice Craig said that the traveller who sees it for the first time 'feels as … if he were to stumble unawares upon the monstrous silences of Karnak or Luxor.' Now largely out of public view, this is probably the finest Victorian exterior in Dublin. With an Egyptian theme on the facade, this terminus of the Midland Great Western Railway (MGWR) was completed in 1850 to a design by John Skipton Mulvany.

Right. Colonnade at the east side of Broadstone.

Top and middle left.
Views of the interior of
the Broadstone Station
building (now the head-
quarters of Bus Éireann,
Ireland's national bus
service).

Left. Old buildings at the
former MGWR Broad-
stone Works.

Above. The Broadstone Station building was the headquarters of the MGWR, whose coat of arms graces a marble fire-place there.

Right. The interior of the building at Broadstone Station is as impressive as the exterior, and executed in a heroic style. Here can be seen one of the grand doorways flanked by a Doric column.

Below. One of the Ionic columns of the colonnade at Broadstone Station. The colonnade dates from 1861.

Above. Plain yet elegant. In this view from the 1980s, the former railway station at Dundrum on the Harcourt Street line.

Left. Harcourt Street Station, one of the five railway termini of Victorian Dublin. It opened in 1859. The design, in Roman Baroque, was by George Wilkinson.

Left. Sandstone on brown brick: the harmonious oval windows at Harcourt Street Station.

Left. A wrought-iron roof-truss spans the track and platforms at Amiens Street (now Connolly) Station. Red-brick walls with yellow-brick arches form the perimeter.

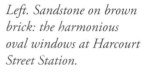

Right. Company crest of the Dublin & South Eastern Railway. The arms of Dublin (in the centre) are surrounded by those of Wicklow, Wexford, New Ross and Waterford.

Above. The former station building at Kingstown, (now Dún Laoghaire) which was completed in 1854. It was designed by John Skipton Mulvany in the neo-classical style that he used for his two adjacent Royal Irish and Royal St. George Yacht club buildings.

Deane Butler station building with another Italianate tower. On the north side, there is a fine and elaborate example of polychromism. This particular use of patterns of red and yellow brick became a characteristic of GNR(I) station architecture.

The Great Southern & Western Railway (GS&WR) was the line to the south-west. Construction of the line began in 1845. Two eminent men of the Irish railway age were involved. Sir John Macneill was appointed as company engineer. William Dargan's construction company was one of the principal contractors. In August 1846 a service was opened to Carlow, having branched off from what is now known as the 'mainline' at Cherryville. Progress was rapid. Thurles was reached in 1848. By October 1849 Cork had a railway service using a temporary terminus located to the north of the city. The GS&WR headquarters and station at Kingsbridge (now Heuston Station) proclaims a date of 1844 but the architect for the building was selected by competition only in 1845. The building was completed in 1848. The station is imposing and dominates its location by the Liffey. The design, by the English architect Sancton Wood, employs decorative carvings and Corinthian pillars and balustrades. There is a hint of India about the cupolas on either side of the building. Such eastern exoticism was not unknown in the Dublin of these years. In the adjacent bridge at Kingsbridge, an Egyptian theme was applied to the abutments, and was also used at Broadstone Station. The front of the Kingsbridge Station accommodated the company administrative offices. Córas Iompair Éireann (CIÉ, the Irish transport company) Board meetings are now

Above. Harp and shamrock carvings atop a limestone column supporting the elevated Loop Line at Beresford Place. Requests were made during construction of the controversial line to improve ornamentation and substitute stone for iron at the abutments.

Left. The Liffey Viaduct was constructed as part of the Loop Line, which opened in 1891. With cast-iron pillars and steel trusses, it represents late-Victorian engineering in all its solidity. It offers a jarring contrast to the classicism of Gandon's Custom House, many views of which it managed to block.

Right. Highly-decorated columns of the bridge at the front of Pearse Station.

Above. Westland Row (now Pearse) Station. This was Dublin's first railway station, the city terminus of the Dublin & Kingstown Railway of 1834. The station was altered when the Loop Line connection over the Liffey and the streets of central Dublin, to Amiens Street (now Connolly) Station was constructed,

held in what was the GS&WR boardroom. The operational part of the station is at the rear. The platforms are covered by a large roof supported by cast-iron columns. This, one of the largest examples of early railway roof-spans, was designed by Macneill. Dargan was the contractor and the ironwork was supplied by J. & R. Mallet of Dublin.

In the early 1840s a railway from Dublin to the west, to serve Athlone, with a branch to Longford, was proposed. An Act was passed in 1845 that enabled the Midland Great Western Railway (MGWR) to begin construction. The Act also authorised the company to purchase the Royal Canal. The first part of the MGWR was to be built at the side of the Royal Canal, following it closely for nearly 60 kilometres out of Dublin. Services to Kinnegad began in 1847 and to Mullingar in 1848. By 1847, the company had been authorised to extend to Galway and services to there began in 1851.

John Skipton Mulvany was engaged to design many of the company's stations. His outstanding monument in Dublin is the station at Broadstone. The building was completed in 1850, with the eastern colonnade being added in 1861. This striking building dominates the plateau of open space where once the Royal Canal harbour lay. The frontage has vestiges of an Egyptian theme. At the western side of the station were the departure platforms; on the eastern side the long neo-classical colonnade. The station provided a graceful welcoming

Left. A view from the 1980s: the Point Depot was a railway freight depot with sidings and timber-floored galleries equipped with small cranes.

Right. A view from on high: the receding lines of the trussed roof of the Point Depot, as it looked before its conversion to an entertainment venue. It was constructed in 1878 to handle sundry freight from the nearby Dublin Port.

Left. Classical and re-strained limestone and red brick, the exterior of the Point Depot as it was in the 1980s. It has since been redeveloped to be-come the O$_2$ venue.

sight of Victorian Dublin for travellers from the west. None can better Maurice Craig's description of the building in his *Dublin 1660-1860*: 'The Broadstone ... is the last building in Dublin to partake of the sublime. Its lonely grandeur is emphasised now by its disuse as a terminus ... It stands on rising ground, and the traveller who sees it for the first time, so unexpected in its massive amplitude, feels a little as he might if he were to stumble unawares upon the monstrous silences of Karnak or Luxor.' It is sad that the station, probably the city's pre-eminent Victorian building, is located in a backwater largely out of public view. In addition to its architectural splendour, the location is a poignant testimony to Dublin's transport connections, past and present. It was a terminus for both the canal and the railway. Last used as a railway station in 1937, it now serves as the headquarters of the national bus company, Bus Éireann. Broadstone's architect designed many other railway buildings including the original station at Athlone. Another railway station by Mulvany is that at Kingstown (now Dún Laoghaire), completed in 1854. The granite building is no longer in use as a station and now serves as a restaurant. Mulvany also designed the equally classical, but smaller, station at Blackrock. The style was also applied in his designs for two yacht clubs at Dún Laoghaire.

A connection south to Wexford with the possibility of cross-channel services spurred consideration of a new railway south of Kingstown. The D&KR tried, but failed, to get an Act passed for a connection to Bray. An inland route was mooted and, in 1851, the Dublin & Wicklow Railway (D&WR) was empowered to build a railway from Dundrum to Bray and also from Dalkey to Bray. Another company, the Dublin & Bray Railway (D&BR), began work on the Dublin to Dundrum section. It was not successful and, in 1853, the D&WR took over the D&BR line. In July 1854, the first train service operated from a temporary station at Harcourt Road to Bray and also from Bray to Dalkey.

The Kingstown to Sandycove atmospheric section had been rebuilt for the passage of steam trains. The great English engineer, Isambard Kingdom Brunel, was involved with the works underway on the line south of Bray. Timber trestle

Above. The London & North Western Railway (L&NWR) Station at North Wall quay, which allowed a direct link with steamship services. Connections could be made from here to the south, west and north of the country. The L&NWR was the largest railway in Britain or Ireland up to 1923.

Right. The L&NWR operated cross-channel steamers to Ireland. From 1877, it operated services from the North Wall to Holyhead. This imposing building on the quayside at North Wall was the former L&NWR hotel, adjacent to the station there.

Right. Insignia of the L&NWR in red terra-cotta at the former hotel on North Wall.

Left. Terraced coastguard houses at Pigeon House Road, Ringsend.

Right. The former Tropical Fruit Warehouse on Sir John Rogerson's Quay, dating from around 1890. The stone heads over the doors, carved by Edward Smyth, had been keystones in the original 1795 Carlisle Bridge over the Liffey. This was reconstructed in 1880 and is now known as O'Connell Bridge.

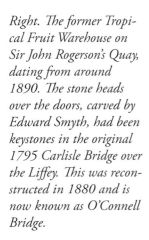

Right. The Rory O'More Bridge over the Liffey, which dates from 1863. The 29-metre single-span bridge was originally called the Victoria and Albert Bridge. One of the earlier bridges here was constructed in timber and known as Bloody Bridge. The cast-iron arches were supplied by Robert Daglish of St. Helen's Foundry in Lancashire.

Above. The graceful stepped and curving lines of the Graving Dock at the North Wall of Dublin Port as seen in the 1980s. Constructed in granite by William Dargan in 1859, it was founded on piles of timber which came from Memel in Prussia (now Klaipeda in Lithuania).

Left. A view of the Graving Dock, in 2009. It was filled in in 2010.

Right. Dublin Port engineer, Bindon Blood Stoney, devised an innovative way of using 360-ton blocks of concrete to build the quay walls during the extension to the port which began in 1871. This diving bell was used to allow workmen to prepare the harbour bed.

Right. This lighthouse was originally constructed in 1881 and moved to its present location on the North Wall extension in 1937.

Below. Dublin Port, and to the right, the North Bank lighthouse, which replaced a nearby earlier lighthouse, known as the Beacon light, in 1940.

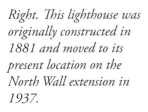

viaducts and tunnels were required along the difficult Bray Head section. As with the later Vartry Water Scheme, Victorian engineering was required on a truly heroic scale to traverse the rugged parts of County Wicklow. By 1855, there were services between Kingstown and Wicklow. In 1858, a new bridge was constructed by Courtney, Stephens & Bailey to carry the D&WR across the Grand Canal to a new terminus, which was being built at Harcourt Street. The station there, designed by George Wilkinson, opened in 1859. As with Amiens Street and Westland Row stations, the tracks and platforms were built high above road level, as the connecting tracks had to pass over the surrounding streets.

Thus, by 1859, there were five railway termini on the perimeter of the central city. This was an unusually large number and was more suited to Dublin's former glory as second city of the Empire than the more modest position it was to hold during the Victorian era. Not only were the termini located at some distance from each other, but cooperation was not notable among the different railway companies. Several connecting schemes were proposed for a direct link from Westland Row to Kingsbridge. None of the schemes saw the light of day. Successful completion of the present plan for the underground urban rail system from the Docklands, running under the Liffey to St. Stephen's Green and onto Heuston Station, will mark the fulfilment of the grand dream to connect the termini via the River Liffey.

The quickening flow of manufactured goods which were in demand led to pressure for a rail connection with the docks. The *Dublin Builder* noted in 1861 that '160,000 tons of traffic are now carted through Dublin, to the great encumbrance of the streets.' The advantage of a rail connection with the docks would save the 'painful transit of boilers, locomotive engines and rolling-stock made in England and dragged by long teams from the Liffey through the streets to their termini.' The West was linked to the port when the MGWR built a rail connection to the docks in 1864. Like its parent railway, the line followed the Royal Canal all the way to the North Wall. The south of the country was connected to the docks by a GS&WR route, completed in 1877. This line passed over the river Liffey to the north of Kingsbridge, then through a tunnel under the Phoenix Park. It looped around the limits of the developing Victorian city in a great circle, passing through cuttings in Cabra and then joined the MGWR line at Glasnevin.

The London & North Western Railway (L&NWR) operated cross-channel steamers to Ireland and supported the GS&WR moves to connect with the Dublin docks. In 1877 it operated services from Holyhead to Dublin North Wall. The company built a station, sidings and a hotel on the quayside. Direct rail connections could now be made to steamship services from the south, west and north.

Pressure built up for a rail connection to Amiens Street Station from Westland Row. There was obvious benefit to the railway companies in joining these two transport hubs that were located north and south of the Liffey. A scheme for an elevated railway was proposed, to considerable opposition. Dublin Corporation objected to what they saw as the disfigurement of Beresford Place by the new bridges. Representations were made about the need for ornamentation and the substitution of stone for iron in the abutments. Despite

Above. Detail of nine-teenth-century crane at George's Dock.

Below. This city gate was built along the Liffey in 1820 at Bloody Bridge (now the Rory O'More Bridge) to a design by Francis Johnston. It was considered to be blocking the access to the new Kingsbridge railway station and was relocated in 1846 to the western entrance to the Royal Hospital in Kilmainham.

Above. Cast-iron plates, and a touch of rust at the base: the North Bull lighthouse. Following representations from ships' masters, approval was given for this lighthouse at the end of the North Bull Wall in 1871. Despite difficulties encountered in establishing foundations, it was constructed and was lit for the first time in 1880.

all the difficulties, the line was built and the Loop Line opened to traffic in May 1891. One unfortunate result is the railway viaduct over the Liffey which presents its functional soul in the most public of manners. The engineers of the nineteenth century frequently built structures of grandeur. Regrettably, both in its setting and style, this viaduct does not follow that grand tradition and it overshadows Gandon's Custom House, Dublin's finest eighteenth-century building. The bitterness about the building of the Loop Line persisted. In 1939 the trade unionist James Larkin alleged that 'A tunnel would have been constructed years ago were it not that the Unionists and the Irish Parliamentary Party were influenced to agree to the erection of the Loop Line.'

The Vikings chose to settle in Dublin because of its strategic location and also for its harbour. It developed as a prosperous trading port throughout medieval times and beyond. As the port grew, there were continuous difficulties in navigating the shallow waters of the estuary with its ragged shoreline. From early times, banks and walls were built to provide docking for ships. Over the centuries, continual improvements were necessary to allow larger ships to access the port. A significant advance was achieved at the dawn of the nineteenth century with the creation of two great sea walls at the port entrance. The South Bull Wall, completed in 1795, stretches out into the bay from Ringsend. The North Bull Wall was completed by the 1820s. The concept behind the two great sea walls was that the natural scour of the outflowing tide would deepen the river and its approaches. This worked and the silt, which would have been deposited on the river approaches, was now carried northwards to form the Bull Island.

At the start of the Victorian era, Dublin Port grew in importance as one of the principal channels of trade for Ireland. The Industrial Revolution was providing a supply of relatively cheap manufactured goods from the burgeoning factories in Britain. One of the most significant factors that boosted trade throughout the nineteenth century was the emergence of new, efficient forms of transport. The construction of an extensive network of railways in Ireland and Britain, improvements in port facilities, and the development of steamships meant that goods could be transported cheaply and quickly, with Dublin being a major hub for trade to and from Ireland.

The construction of the North Bull Wall greatly improved the depth of channel available to shipping. George's Docks (now part of the Irish Financial Services Centre area) were opened in 1821. However, these docks were found to be unsatisfactory after they opened. The entrance locks proved too small for larger ships that came into service in following years. In 1815, the first steamship had sailed into the port. As the century progressed, this innovative form of sea transport gradually became the dominant form of shipping in the port. Most cross-channel shipping was propelled by steam after 1860.

Freight traffic through the port grew substantially. From 1840 to 1860, the annual tonnage doubled to a figure of one million tons. By 1880, there was a throughput of over two million tons. At this time, Dublin was the largest port in the country and had a greater rate of growth than the ports of Liverpool and Glasgow. Overseas shipping accounted for only a small proportion of the total and Dublin in time became a port mainly handling overseas goods which were transhipped in smaller vessels from large cross-channel ports such as Liverpool. By 1900, Dublin had lost its ranking and Belfast had grown to become Ireland's biggest port.

Post-Famine Ireland saw a decline in tillage and a corresponding rise in cattle raising. Cattle exporting became a large and lucrative business in Dublin port. The pattern of trade reflected Ireland's colonial status. In what is a typical third-world pattern of today, nineteenth-century Ireland exported its raw materials, such as live cattle, and received manufactured goods in return. One major exception to this were the rapidly-expanding exports from Guinness and other Dublin breweries.

During the early part of Victoria's reign, the quays extended down to the area around what is now the East Link bridge. As ships grew in size, various timber wharves were built in an attempt to cater for the ever-growing demand. In the 1860s, it was decided to begin construction of the first deep-water quays. These extended seawards along the North Wall. The work began in 1871, under the guidance of the gifted port engineer Bindon Blood Stoney. He devised an innovative method whereby the massive quay walls were built quickly and efficiently. A diving bell was used to allow workmen to excavate and level the harbour bed. Massive blocks of precast concrete, 360 tons in weight, were placed by a steam-operated floating crane. This technique was efficient and fast and avoided the need for cofferdams, which at that time was the usual method of constructing quays. Cross-channel steamers could now sail independently of the tide and larger overseas vessels could use the port.

As the nineteenth century ended, a substantial transport infrastructure was in place in Dublin. A significantly-improved port was connected to the railways, which radiated across Ireland. The railways were soon to reach their apogee, followed by rapid contraction, which occurred during the next century. Within the city itself, citizens enjoyed easy and rapid access to the new suburbs of the late-Victorian city, travelling on electric trams or suburban railways. The rise of the internal combustion engine and the decline of the trams came in the twentieth century and led to gridlock on the city streets by that century's end. It remains to be seen if, in the future, the present renaissance of the tram and other public transport can help recreate the easy access that was a characteristic of Dublin at the end of the Victorian era.

Bibliography

For those who wish to explore Victorian Dublin further, the following are recommended, in the first instance:

Casey, C., *The Buildings of Ireland; Dublin*, Yale University Press, New Haven and London, 2005.

Daly, M. E., *Dublin, the Deposed Capital*, Cork University Press, Cork, 1985.

Ó Maitiú, S., *Dublin's Suburban Towns 1834-1930*, Four Courts Press, Dublin, 2003.

Williams, J., *A Companion Guide to Architecture in Ireland, 1837-1921*, Irish Academic Press, Dublin, 1994.

Other sources:

A Social and Natural History of Sandymount, Irishtown, Ringsend, Sandymount Community Services, Dublin, 1993.

Aalen, F. H., Whelan, K., *Dublin, City and County: From Prehistory to Present*, Geography Publications, Dublin 1992.

Barry, M., *Across Deep Waters, Bridges of Ireland*, Frankfort Press, Dublin, 1985.

Barry, M., *Restoring a Victorian House*, Frankfort Press, Dublin, 1988.

Barry, M., *Tales of the Permanent Way*, Andalus Press, Dublin, 2009.

Barry, M., *Through the Cities, The Revolution in Light Rail*, Frankfort Press, Dublin, 1991.

Bartlett, T., Jeffery, K., Ed., *A Military History of Ireland*, Cambridge University Press, Cambridge, 1996.

Beckett, J. C., *The Making of Modern Ireland 1603-1923*, Faber & Faber, London, 1972.

Bowers, M., *Dublin City Parks and Gardens*, Lilliput Press, Dublin, 1999.

Brady, J., Simms, A., Ed, *Dublin Through Space and Time*, Four Courts Press, Dublin 2001.

Clapham, J. H., *An Economic History of Modern Britain*, Cambridge University Press, Cambridge, 1967.

Cooke, P., *A History of Kilmainham Gaol*, Stationery Office, Dublin, 1995.

Connell, C., *Glasnevin Cemetery, Dublin, 1832-1900*, Four Courts Press, Dublin, 2004.

Connolly, S. J., Ed., *The Oxford Companion to Irish History*, Oxford University Press, Oxford, 1998.

Corcoran, M., *Through Streets Broad and Narrow, a History of Dublin Trams*, Midland Publishing, Leicester 2000.

Corcoran, M., *Our Good Health*, Dublin City Council, Dublin, 2005.

Cosgrave, D., *North Dublin*, Nonsuch, Dublin, 2005.

Costello, P., *Dublin Churches*, Gill and Macmillan, Dublin, 1989.

Cox, R., *Civil Engineering at Trinity*, University of Dublin, Dublin, 2009.

Cox, R., *Engineering Ireland*, Collins Press, Cork, 2006.

Cox, R., *Robert Mallet, F.R.S., 1810-1881*, Institution of Engineers of Ireland, Dublin, 1982.

Craig, M., *Dublin 1660-1860*, Allen Figgis, Dublin, 1980.

Craig, M., *The Architecture of Ireland*, Batsford, London, 1983.

Cullen, L. M., *An Economic History of Ireland since 1660*, Batsford, London, 1972.

Cullen, L. M., Ed., *The Formation of the Irish Economy*, Mercier Press, Cork, 1969.

Curtis, J., *Times Chimes & Charms of Dublin*, Verge Books, Dublin, 1992.

Daly, M., Hearn, M., Pearson, P., *Dublin's Victorian Houses*, A. & A. Farmar, 1998.

Daly, M., *Social and Economic History of Ireland since 1800*, The Educational Company, Dublin, 1981.

Delany, R., *Ireland's Inland Waterways*, Appletree Press, Belfast, 1986.

De Courcy, J. W., *The Liffey in Dublin*, Gill and Macmillan, Dublin 1996.

De Courcy Ireland, J., *History of Dún Laoghaire Harbour*, Caisleán an Bhúrcaigh, Dublin, 2001.

Dixon, R., Muthesius, S., *Victorian Architecture*, Thames and Hudson, London, 1978.

Doyle, O., Hirsch, S., *Railways in Ireland 1834-1984*, Signal Press, Dublin, 1983.

Fleetwood, J. F., *The History of Medicine in Ireland*, Skellig Press, Dublin, 1983.

Gilligan, H. A., *A History of the Port of Dublin*, Gill and Macmillan, Dublin 1989.

Glass, I. S., *Victorian Telescope Makers, The Lives and letters of Thomas and Howard Grubb*, Institute of Physics Publishing, Bristol, 1997.

Gorham, M., *Dublin from Old Photographs*, Batsford, London, 1972.

Guedalla, P., *The Duke*, Woodsworth Editions, Ware, 1997.

Hill, R., *God's Architect*, Penguin Books, London, 2007.

Hunt, T., *Building Jerusalem*, Metropolitan Books, New York, 2005.

Igoe, V., *Dublin Burial Grounds and Graveyards*, Wolfhound Press, Dublin, 2001.

Jackson, V., *The Monuments in St. Patrick's Cathedral*, Dublin, 1987.

Johnston, L., *Dublin then and now*, Gill and Macmillan, Dublin 1989.

Kelly, D., *Four Roads to Dublin*, O'Brien Press, Dublin, 2001.

Kennedy, R., *Dublin Castle Art*, Office of Public Works, Dublin, 1999.

Kennedy, T., Ed., *Victorian Dublin*, Albertine Kennedy Publishing, Dublin, 1980.

Lalor, B., *Dublin Bay from Killiney to Howth*, O'Brien Press, Dublin 1989.

Langtry, J., Carter, N., Ed, *Mount Jerome, a Victorian Cemetery*, Staybro Publications, Dublin, 1997.

Lee, J., *The Modernisation of Irish Society 1848-1918*, Gill and Macmillan, Dublin, 2008.

Liddy, P., *Dublin be Proud*, Chadworth, Dublin, 1987.

Lyons, F. S., *Ireland Since the Famine*, Weidenfeld and Nicolson, 1971.

Lyons, F. S., Hawkins, R. A. J., Ed, *Ireland Under the Union*, Clarendon Press, Oxford, 1980.

Malone, A., *Historic Pubs of Dublin*, New Island, Dublin, 2001.

McCarthy, D., *Dublin Castle*, Stationery Office, Dublin, 2004.

McCullough, N., *Dublin, An Urban History*, Anne Street Press, Dublin, 1989.

MacDonagh, O., *Ireland, the Union and its Aftermath*, UCD Press, Dublin 1977.

MacLoughlin, A., *Guide to Historic Dublin*, Gill and Macmillan, Dublin, 1979.

Marshall, D., *The Life and Times of Victoria*, Weidenfeld and Nicholson, London, 1972.

Mulvihill, M., *Ingenious Ireland*, TownHouse, Dublin, 2002.

Nolan, B., *Phoenix Park*, Liffey Press, Dublin, 2006.

Nuttgens, P., *The Story of Architecture*, Phaidon Press, Oxford, 1985.

Ó Broin, L., *Fenian Fever*, Chatto & Windus, London, 1971.

O'Connell, A., *The Servant's Church, A History of the Church of the Three Patrons in the Parish of Rathgar*, Parish Development Group, Dublin 2004.

Ó Gráda, C., *Ireland, a New Economic History, 1780-1939*, Clarendon Press, Oxford, 1994.

Ó Gráda, C., *Jewish Ireland in the Age of Joyce*, Princeton University Press, Princeton, 2006.

O'Meara, L., *Within & Without ... Dublin Churches of St. Nicholas*, Riposte Books, Dublin, 2008.

O'Shea, S., *Death and Design in Victorian Glasnevin*, Dublin Cemeteries Committee, Dublin 2000.

O'Sullivan, C. J., *The Gasmakers, Historical Perspectives on the Irish Gas Industry*, The O'Brien Press, Dublin, 1987.

Pakenham, T. & V., *Dublin, a Travellers' Companion*, Constable, London, 1998.

Pearson, P., *Between the Mountains and the Sea*, O'Brien Press, Dublin, 2001.

Pearson, P., *The Heart of Dublin*, O'Brien Press, Dublin 2000.

Póirtéir, C., *The Great Irish Famine*, Mercier Press, Cork, 1995.

Prunty, J., *Dublin Slums, 1800-1925*, Irish Academic Press, Dublin, 2000.

Ross, D., *Ireland, History of a Nation*, Geddes & Grosset, Scotland, 2009.

Ryan, G., *The Works*, Dublin, 1996.

Rynne, C., *Industrial Ireland 1750-1930*, Collins Press, 2006.

Sammon, P., *Greenspeak*, TownHouse, Dublin, 2002.

Shaw, H., *The Dublin Pictorial Guide & Directory of 1850*, The Friar's Bush Press, Belfast, 1988.

Sheaff, N., *Iveagh House*, Department of Foreign Affairs, Dublin, 1978.

Shepherd, E., Beesley, G., *Dublin & South Eastern Railway*, Midland Publishing, Leicester, 1998.

Shepherd, E., *The Midland Great Western Railway of Ireland*, Midland Publishing, Leicester, 1994.

Somerville-Large, P, *Dublin*, Granada Publishing, St. Albans 1979.

St. John Joyce, W., *The Neighbourhood of Dublin*, Hughes and Hughes, Dublin 1994

Townsend, B., *The Lost Distilleries of Ireland*, Neil Wilson Publishing, Glasgow, 1999.

Vaughan, W. E., *A New History of Ireland*, Oxford University Press, Oxford, 1989.

Wayman, P., *Dunsink Observatory, 1785-1985*, RDS, Dublin 1987.

Wilson, A. N., *The Victorians*, Arrow Books, London, 2002

Woodham-Smith, C., *Queen Victoria*, Knopf, New York, 1972.

Index

Abbey Theatre 36
Act of Union 18, 22, 50, 118, 122
Adams, Robert 44
Adelaide Road 31
AIB 145, 156
Ailesbury Road 110
Albert Edward, Prince of Wales 106
All Hallows College 113
Alliance and Dublin Consumers' Gas Company140
Amiens Street (now Connolly) Station 138, 166, 174, 170, 177
Anglesea Street 150
Antient Concert Rooms 36, 142
Arbour Hill 15, 90
Ardilaun, Lord 122, 126
Arnott & Company 156
Arnotts 70
Arnott, Sir John 156
Arran Quay 82
Ashlin, George 32, 84, 87, 100
Aston Quay 160
Athy 160
Atmospheric Railway 165
Australia 138

Baggot Street 40, 153
Baggot Street Hospital 32
Balbriggan 170
Ballsbridge 62, 63, 65, 110, 138
Barrack (now Benburb) Street 78
Barrow Street 153
Bath Avenue 65
Belfast 22, 73, 116-118, 137, 138, 148, 154, 166, 170
Belfast Banking Company 148
Belgrave Square, Monkstown 70
Bentley, Mark 70
Beresford Place 176, 186
Berlin 162
Bessborough Parade 55
Betjeman, John 93
Bewley, Moss & Co. Sugar Refinery 137
Bianconi, Charles 160
Birmingham 22, 73
Black Church, St. Mary's Place 99
Blackhall Place 138
Blackhorse Avenue 46
Blackrock 68, 80, 113, 116, 180
Blessington 162
Blessington Basin 43
Bloody Bridge 183, 186
Bohernabreena 61, 119, 122
Bolger, James 86
Botanic Gardens 29
Bourke, John 31, 40
Bow Street 137
Boyd, John McNeill 98
Boyne, Battle of the 82
Bray 36, 74, 180

Bray Head 180
Brighton Vale 72
Britain 117, 118, 120, 137, 158, 187
British Admiralty 138, 142
British Army 44, 46
British Empire 96
Broadstone Station 27, 76, 138, 171-173, 175
Brooks, Maurice, MP 162
Brown Thomas 150, 156
Brunel, Isambard Kingdom 180
Buckingham Palace 48
Bull Alley 80
Burma War 96
Burmantofts 25
Burton, Decimus 43, 138
Bus Éireann 172, 180
Butler, William Deane 167, 170
Byrne, Patrick 82, 86, 90, 95
Byzantine 88, 115

Cabra 186
Camac River 119, 122
Cambi, Carlo 22
Camden Street 154
Capel Street 137
Carlisle Bridge 183
Carmichael School of Medicine 32
Carrickbrennan Road 151
Carrickmines 70
Carroll and Batchelor. 31
Carson, Sir Edward 73
Casey, Christine 86, 90, 95
Cassidy's Public House,
Castle Avenue 74
Castlereagh, Viscount 10
Catholic Association 101, 105
Catholic Church 28, 82
Catholic Emancipation 22, 31, 50, 81, 82, 158
Catholic middle class 82
Catholic nationalism 81
Catholic Relief Act 26
Catholic University 95, 116
Cenotaph of the Julii 123
Central Model School 108
Chatham Street 155
China War 96
Cholera epidemic 38
Christ Church Cathedral 78, 90, 95, 98, 106
Christian Brothers 111
Church of Ireland 82, 99, 102, 116
Church of Ireland Monkstown 93
Church of Saints Augustine and John 85
Church of St. Paul of the Cross, 87
Church of the Three Patrons, Rathgar 90, 95
City Fruit and Vegetable Market 136
Cleary's Public House, Inchicore 153

Clery, J. 156
Cloncurry, Lord 68
Clondalkin 160
Clonliffe College 73
Clonmel 160
Clonsilla 74
Clonskeagh 162
Clontarf 26, 62, 70, 73, 74, 111, 160, 162
Clontarf Castle 74
Clontarf Township 74
Clyde Road 65, 66, 105
Coffey, Aeneas 130
College Green 46, 143, 145, 146, 160
College of Education, Carysfort 113
College Street 13, 132, 143, 154
Commercial Union Assurance Co. 143
Congress of Vienna 10
Coombe 78
Córas Iompair Éireann 175
Corrigan, Sir Dominic 29, 44
Cork 116, 175
Cork Street 31
Courtney, Stephens & Bailey 130, 138, 186
Covent Garden 128
Craig, Maurice 95, 171, 177
Crimean War 96, 97, 138
Crosthwaite Park 132
Crown Life Insurance 156
Cullen, Cardinal Paul 73, 111
Curran, John Philpot 102
Curvilinear Range, Glasnevin 20, 138
Custom House 176, 187

Daglish, Robert 183
D'Arcy's Anchor Brewery 130
D'Olier Street, 147
Dalkey 68, 70, 80, 162, 165, 166
Dame Court 156
Dame Street 143, 146, 147, 154, 156
Dan Lowry's Music Hall (Olympia) 36
Dargan, William 22, 29, 164, 165, 168, 175, 184
Dargle River 59
Darley, F., 108
Darwin, Charles 26
Davis, Thomas 111
Dawson Street 95, 151
Deane, Sir Thomas 40, 115, 156
Deane, Sir Thomas Manly 22, 25, 143
Deane, Thomas Newenham 143, 145, 156
Deane and Woodward 38, 108. 115
Deane, T. N. and T. M. 28, 147
Dental Hospital 32
Department of Foreign Affairs 126
Dodder 119, 122

Doheny and Nesbitt's Public House 153
Dolphin's Barn 74
Donnybrook 134
Drew, Thomas 113, 146, 156
Dr. Steeven's Hospital 31
Drogheda 170
Drumcondra 46, 100, 162
Dublin & Drogheda Railway 138, 166, 167
Dublin & Kingstown Railway 38, 70, 137, 138, 164, 166, 177
Dublin & South Eastern Railway 174
Dublin & Wicklow Railway 180
Dublin Artisans' Dwelling Company, 78
Dublin Builder 52, 70, 186
Dublin Castle 28, 36
Dublin Corporation 28, 50, 55, 61, 68, 70, 73, 78, 82, 140, 142, 153, 156, 160, 186
Dublin Docks 120
Dublin Drapery Warehouse 156
Dublin Electric Light Company 153
Dublin Metropolitan Police 43
Dublin Oil Gas Company 142
Dublin Port 159, 179, 184, 185, 187
Dublin South Eastern Railway Company 68
Dublin Southern District Tramways Company 162
Dublin United Tramways Company 162
Dublin Whiskey Distillery 129, 137
Dublin Working Boys' Home and Harding Technical School 108, 110
Dublin Zoo 18
Dublin, Wicklow & Wexford Railway Company 162
Dún Laoghaire 44, 46, 68, 69, 70, 80, 98, 132, 164-166, 180
Dundrum 174
Dunsink Observatory 18, 138

Earlsfort Terrace 132
East Link Bridge 188
Eccles Street 31
Edinburgh 100
Eglinton Road 134
Egypt 34
Elgin Road 66, 68, 80
Essex Quay 136
Exhibition of Art and Industry, 1853 29, 165

Fairview 74
Farmleigh 125
Fenians, 26, 155
First World War 138, 142
Fitzwilliam Estate 50, 61
Fitzwilliam Square 50, 73
Fleet Street 153

Foley, John Henry 13
Foster Place 145
Four Courts 86
Fownes Street 147, 156
Foxrock 70
Francis Street 84, 86
Franciscan Church of the Immaculate Conception 82
Franco-Prussian War 118
Franklin Expedition 98
Freeman's Journal 153, 162
Freemasons' Hall 34, 67, 106

Gaiety Theatre 36, 42
Galway 116, 177
Gardiner Estate 50
Garville Avenue 160
George's Docks 188
George's Street Arcade 148
Georgian Dublin 50
Glasgow 188
Glasnevin 20, 78, 102, 111, 138, 186
Glasnevin Cemetery 101, 105, 111, 153
Glenasmole Valley 61
Gospel Hall, Upper Rathmines Road 99
Goulding, W. & H. M. 122
Graduates' Memorial Building 113
Grafton Street 143
Grand Canal 38, 50, 68, 160, 186
Grand Canal Company 61
Grand Canal Docks 137
Grand Canal Quay, 137
Grand Canal Street 137
Grantham Street 107
Grattan Bridge 138, 160
Graving Dock 184
Gray, Sir John 61
Great Britain 10
Great Brunswick (now Pearse) Street 36, 142
Great Famine 29, 44, 86, 158, 188
Great Mosque of Córdoba 115
Great Northern Railway (Ireland) 167, 168, 170
Great Palm House, Kew 138
Great Southern & Western Railway 73, 77, 137, 138, 153, 164, 168, 175
Great Western Square 76
Gregory, Lady 36
Gresham tomb 102
Griffith, Richard 40
Grosvenor Road 108
Grubb Optical and Mechanical Works 18, 125, 142, 138
Guinness 122, 130, 188
Guinness, Arthur 128
Guinness Brewery 120
Guinness, Sir Benjamin Lee 122, 123, 126
Gulistan 78

Haddington Road 162

Hague, William 110
Hamilton, William Rowan 111
Harcourt Road 180
Harcourt Street 119, 174
Harcourt Street Station 174
Hardwick, P. C. 38
Harold's Cross 55, 78
Harrison, Charles 40, 146
Harry Street 142
Harvie memorial 102
Hawkins Street 153
Henry Street 153
Hibernian Bank 146
High Street 82
HMS 'Ajax', 98
HMS 'Enterprise' 98
Hodges Figgis 151
Holy Trinity Church, Rathmines 93
Holyhead 180
Holmes, Edward 34
Hong Kong 96
Houghton House 18
House of Commons 165
Howth 170
Howth Castle 134
Hutton's 118

Iarnród Éireann 167
Imperial Royal Observatory of Austro-Hungary 138
Inchicore 78, 130, 132, 137, 169, 170
India 10, 97
Indian Mutiny 96
Irish College, Rome 111
Irish Financial Services Centre 188
Irish International Exhibition, 1872 132
Irish Stock Exchange 154
Irish Times 95
Irishtown 68
Islandbridge 43
Islandbridge (Clancy) Barracks 16
Iveagh House 126
Iveagh, Lord 80, 125
Iveagh Trust 80

Jacob, W. & R. 137
James Weir Home for Nurses 31
James's Street 87, 130, 160
Jameson Distillery 128, 137
Jameson, George 106
Jebb, Joshua 15
Jervis Street Hospital 32, 44
Jewish Synagogue, Adelaide Road 99
John's Lane 137
Johnston, Francis 186
Johnston, Mooney & O'Brien 137
Jones' s Road 129, 137
Joseph Adamson & Co. 170
Joyce, James 38

Karnak 171, 180
Kavanagh's Public House 153

Keane, J. B. 82, 87
Kenilworth Square 54
Khyber Pass 97
Kildare Street 153
Kildare Street Club 38, 40, 41, 134
Killiney 68, 70, 80, 138
Killiney Bay 68
Kilmainham 73, 119
Kilmainham Gaol 15, 156
Kingsbridge 186
Kingsbridge (now Heuston) Station 138, 164, 168, 169, 175, 186
Kingstown 36, 44, 46, 48, 68, 70, 74, 98, 164, 165, 166, 180, 186
Kingstown Township 69
Kinnegad 177

Lanyon and Lynn 111
Lanyon, John 167
Lanyon, Sir Charles 113
Larkin, James 187
Le Fanu, Sheridan 111
Leeson, John 84, 86
Leinster House 22, 29
Leinster Lawn 13, 29, 165
Leitrim 27
Liberties 38, 50
Liffey 38, 40, 50, 80, 120, 122, 175, 183, 186
Liffey Viaduct 176
Limerick 169
Lincoln Place 151
Liverpool 22, 188
Liverpool & Lancashire Insurance Company 147
Livingstone, David 26
Lombard, J. 70
London 18, 50, 100, 105, 128
London & North Western Railway 180, 186
Londonbridge Road 61
Longford 177
Long Hall Public House, 155
Loop Line 176, 186, 187
Lord Lieutenant 28, 36
Lower Rathmines Road 138
Lucan 162
Luxor 171, 180

Macneill, John 40, 166, 175
Malahide 167, 170
Malakoff 96
Mallet, John & Robert 38, 132, 138, 168, 177
Manchester 22
Manders & Powell 130
Mansion House 36
Marlborough (now McKee) Barracks 16, 46
Marlborough Street 82, 108
Marlborough Street 111
Marrowbone Lane 137
Mary Immaculate Church, Rathmines 55, 90, 95
Mary Street 148
Masonic Girls' School 66, 110

Mater Misericordiae Hospital 31, 40
Mathew, Father 130
Mathias, Henry 98
Maynooth 87
McCabe, Cardinal 100
McCarthy, J. J. 86, 87, 110
McCurdy, John 156
McDonnell, R. 44
McGeough Home 32
Meath Hospital 31
Merchants' Quay 82
Merrion Square 165
Methodist 108
Methodist Church, Dolphin's Barn 98
Midland Great Western Railway 76, 80, 137, 171-3, 177
Milltown Viaduct 119
Molesworth Street 34, 67
Molloy's Public House 154
Monkstown 70, 72, 73, 80, 99, 151
Moravian Church, Kevin Street 98
Morrison, William Vitruvius 74
Mount Anville 165
Mount Argus 74, 87
Mount Jerome Cemetery 101, 102, 105, 111
Mount Pleasant 55
Mount Temple School 111
Mountjoy Gaol 15
Mountjoy Square 73, 97
Mullingar 177
Mulvany, John Skipton 44, 171, 175
Munster Bank 145, 154
Murphy, William Martin 162
Museum Building 115, 116, 156
Museum of Economic Geology 142

Napoleonic Wars 10, 44
Nassau Street 132
National Bank 145, 154
National Board of Education 107, 116
National College of Art and Design 129
National Concert Hall 132
National Gallery 22, 29, 165
National Library 28, 29, 106
National Museum 24, 25, 29
National Transport Museum, Howth 162
National University of Ireland 116
Natural History Museum 22, 26, 27
Neary's Public House 155
Nelson Pillar (The) 153, 162
Neville, Parke 40, 136
New Ross 174
New York 160
New Zealand War 97
Newman House 116
Newman, John Henry 88, 95, 116
NIB 146
North Bank lighthouse 185

North Brunswick Street 32
North Bull lighthouse 187
North Bull Wall 187, 188
North Circular Road 162
North Strand 74, 107
North Wall 122, 137, 180, 183, 184, 186, 188
Northern Bank 154, 156
Northumberland Road 66, 108

O'Brien Institute, Marino 113
O'Callaghan, J. J. 99, 150
O'Casey, Seán 38
O'Connell Bridge 183
O'Connell, Daniel 22, 101, 105, 116, 142, 145, 154
O'Connell Monument 13
O'Shea Brothers 40, 115, 116
O₂ Venue 179
Observatory Lane 142
Office of Public Works 138, 142
Olympia Theatre 42
Opium War 96
Ordnance Survey, Phoenix Park 132
Owen, E. Trevor 15
Oxford Museum of Natural History 40, 115
Oxford University 116

Palace Bar 153
Palace Street 156
Palm House, Belfast 138
Palmerston Park 57
Papworth, George 102
Paris 26, 82, 157
Parke, Thomas Heazle 27
Parnell, Charles Stewart 169
Parnell Square 105, 106
Partridge, John 48
Pasley, Major-General 166
Pearse Station 166
Pearse Street 110
Pembroke, Earl of 68
Pembroke Estate 61
Pembroke Road 68
Pembroke Town Hall 63
Pembroke Township 50, 61, 63, 65, 68
Penal Laws 82
Penneys 148
Pentonville 15
Peter's Row 137
Phibsboro 80, 119
Phoenix Park 10, 15, 29, 36, 43, 125, 186
Pigeon House 61, 140, 153
Pigeon House Road 183
Point Depot 179
Pollen, John Hungerford 88, 95
Portmarnock 166
Portobello (now Cathal Brugha) Barracks 17, 46
Portrane Asylum (now St. Ita's Hospital) 32, 77, 132

Poulaphuca 162
Power's Distillery 128, 129, 137
Presbyterian 82
Presbyterian Christ Church, Rathgar 98
Prince's Street 153
Pro-Cathedral, 82, 111
Prospect Square 153
Protestant middle class 81
Protestantism 48
Provincial Bank 13, 143
Pugin, A. W. 80, 84, 87
Pugin, E. W. 84, 87
Purdy, C. W. 40

Quakers 137
Queen's University 116

Ranelagh 54, 55, 56, 73, 75
Rathfarnham 160
Rathgar 52, 53, 54, 55, 56, 61, 73, 90, 95, 160
Rathgar Avenue 108
Rathgar National School 108
Rathgar Road 96
Rathmines 46, 50, 57, 68, 73, 74, 78, 95, 125, 134, 148, 160
Rathmines Town Hall 25, 51
Rathmines Township 52, 54, 55, 57, 61, 78, 158, 160
Rathmines Urban District Council 54
Richmond Barracks 73
Richmond Hospital 32
Ringsend 68, 140, 183
River Nore 138
Robert Street 120
Roberts House 18
Robinson, J. L. 69
Roe's Distillery 137
Rory O'More Bridge 183
Rotunda 36, 40
Roundwood, County Wicklow 59
Rowerstown Lane 119
Royal (now Collins) Barracks 17, 36
Royal Bank 145
Royal Canal 119, 166, 170, 177, 186
Royal College of Physicians of Ireland 28, 44
Royal Engineers Department 46
Royal Hospital, Kilmainham 186
Royal Irish Academy 38
Royal Irish Regiment 96
Royal Irish Yacht Club 44
Royal Marine Hotel 166
Royal Navy 138
Royal St. George Yacht 175
Royal University 116
Royal Victoria Eye and Ear Hospital 31, 44
Ruskin, John 80, 84, 87, 95
Ruwenzori Mountains 27
Rynd, Francis 44

Sackville (now O'Connell) Street 156
St. Andrew's 86
St. Andrews National Schools 110
St. Ann's Church 95
St. Anne's Park, Raheny. 122, 123, 132
St. Audoen's Church 82, 86
St. Columba's Infant National Schools 107
St. Francis Xavier's Church 82
St. George's, Hardwicke Place 99
St. James's Church 87
St. John the Evangelist, Sandymount 99
St. Kevin's Female National Schools 107
St. Lawrence O'Toole Church 87
St. Mark's Ophthalmic Hospital 44
St. Michael's School 110
St. Nicholas of Myra 84, 85, 86
St. Patrick's Cathedral 67, 97, 90, 96, 98,122
St. Patrick's College 87
St. Paul's, Arran Quay 86
St. Saviour, Dominick Street 87
St. Stephen's Green 40, 43, 95, 116, 126, 142, 153, 156, 186
St. Stephen's Schools 108
St. Vincent's Hospital 40
Salthill 164
Sandymount 61, 65, 68, 162
Schoolhouse Lane 153
Scottish Widows Insurance 143
Semple, John 93, 99
Seringapatam, Siege of 10
Sevastopol 96
Seville Place 87
Shannon 160
Shaw, George Bernard 38
Shelbourne Hotel 156, 157
Shelbourne Road 162
Sheriff Street 130
Shoe Dagon Pagoda, Rangoon 96
Sir John Rogerson's Quay 183
Sisters of Charity 40
Sisters of Mercy 31
Smithfield 128
Smyth,Edward 183
Sorrento Terrace 68
South Africa 138
South Bull Wall, 187
South City Markets 148, 156
South Great George's Street 148, 155, 156
South Lotts Road 140, 153
Soyer, Alexis 36
Spain 40
Stag's Head Public House 156
Stephenson, John 160 Stillorgan 70
Stokes, Frederick 50, 61, 158
Stokes, William 44
Stoney, Bindon Blood 40, 185, 188
Strawberry Beds 125
Street, George Edmund 95

Sunlight Chambers 136
Sweny's Pharmacy 151
Switzer's Department Store 150, 156
Sydney Parade 65
Synod House 95, 106

Talbot Street 154
Terenure 116, 160, 162
Thomas Street 87, 128, 137
Thomastown 138
Thurles 175
Train, George F. 160
Transport Museum, Cultra 164
Trinity College Dublin 113, 116, 132, 138, 145, 156
Tropical Fruit Warehouse 183
Turner's Ironworks 132, 138
Turner, Richard 20, 138

Ulster Bank 146, 154, 156
Union Bank 146
United Irishmen 82
United Kingdom 18
United States 160, 162
University Church 88, 95
University College, Dublin 116
Upper Beechwood Avenue 54, 75
Upper Gardiner Street 86
Upper Rathmines Road 107
Usher Street 130

Vartry Reservoir 59
Vartry Water Scheme 61, 68
Vatican Museum 102
Vernon family 74
Vernon, John 70
Victoria and Albert Bridge 183
Victoria Fountain 46, 69
Victoria, Queen 18, 34, 43, 46, 48, 118, 153, 165
Vignoles, Charles Blacker 38, 165
Vienna 18, 138
Vikings 187
Von Siemens, Werner 162

Walpole, Webb and Bewley 137
Waterford 174
Waterloo Road 68
Wellington, Duke of, 10, 44
Westland Row (now Pearse) Station 177
Wexford 174
Wicklow 174, 186
Wicklow Street 150
Wilde, Oscar 38
Wilde, Sir William 44, 111
Wilkinson, George 174, 186
Wood, Sancton 169, 175
Writers' Museum 106

Zion Church, Rathgar 99
Zoological Gardens 29